D0437373

An Owner's Manual for the Unfinished Soul

Other books by Calvin Miller:

The Singer

The Song

The Finale

The Valiant Papers

The Taste of Joy

A Hunger for Meaning

The Table of Inwardness

A Requiem for Love

The Philippian Fragment

Apples, Snakes and Bellyaches

When the Aardvark Parked on the Ark

The Singreale Chronicles

The Book of Jesus

Walking with Saints

AN
OWNER'S
MANUAL FOR
THE
UNFINISHED

SOUL

CALVIN
MILLER

HAROLD SHAW PUBLISHERS
WHEATON, ILLINOIS

Some pieces in this collection have been previously published in periodicals or books. All rights remain with the author. Among those pieces taken from books are

"No Shot Was Ever Heard" and "Once in Every Universe," from *A Symphony in Sand,* Word Publishing, © 1990 by Calvin Miller. Used by permission of the author.

"Anthem of the Star," from *The Legend of the Brotherstone,* Harper & Row Publishers, © 1985 by Calvin Miller. Used by permission of the author.

Another version of "Tuesday's Cookies" appears in *Drama for Worship,* Volume 4, © 1992 by Word Music (a division of Word Entertainment, Inc.). All rights reserved. Used by permission.

Unless otherwise noted, Scripture quotations are taken from *The Holy Bible, New International Version.* © 1973, 1978, 1984 International Bible Society. Used by permission of Zondervan Publishing House. All rights reserved.

Scripture quotations taken from the King James Version of the Bible are marked KJV.

Copyright © 1997 by Calvin Miller

All rights reserved. No part of this book may be reproduced or transmitted in any form or by any means, electronic or mechanical, including photocopying, recording, or any information storage and retrieval system without written permission from Harold Shaw Publishers, Box 567, Wheaton, Illinois 60189. Printed in the United States of America.

ISBN 0-87788-554-0

Cover design by David LaPlaca

Library of Congress Cataloging-in-Publication Data

Miller, Calvin.
    An owner's manual for the unfinished soul / Calvin Miller.
      p. cm.
    ISBN 0-87788-554-0 (cloth)
    I. Title.
    PS3563.I376092 1997
    811'.54—dc21   96-37642

04 03 02 01 00 99 98 97

10 9 8 7 6 5 4 3 2 1

Contents

INTRODUCTION

The following bits and pieces of my life have been collected from years of journals and small articles written for newspapers, magazines, and other publications. These collectibles are the overspillings of both the smallest and the most significant moments of my life. Here lie the emotional tracks of my trek toward meaning—my reactions to the various events and ideas with which I have collided.

These vignettes are short. But then life is rarely an orderly compilation of large blocks of time. It is composed mostly of small, ill-fitting happenstances. Life is not an architectural wonder made possible by meticulous blueprints. Rather, it is a jumbled edifice: a collage of little renovations to dreams that must constantly be repaired.

So here is a composite of my significant scrapes and bruises my day-to-day gatherings of short, significant encounters. This book is my admission that it was never during the long lectures at the university or graduate school that I learned the greatest truths. I have never stalked life and tamed it to make it usable. I have always collided with it. Scraped knees, nuclear explosions, amoebas in culture, cotton candy, and the church: all these weird and different items without framework or category have been my motley host of unlikely tutors. Some of these lessons came in the short proverbs of friends who tossed them to me as we passed in the hurried corridors of my sixty years. The counsel that still serves me best in life is that which initially came flying at me over sickbeds or coffee cups.

Further, the most memorable insights were usually sudden and intrusive. These insights forced their way into my already crowded schedule: they were impatient with me and never apologized for being abrupt. I have learned best under such confrontational tutors. Lessons that shock us are unforgettable. I rarely noticed I was on a one-way road until I met with head-on traffic. My best friends were those who halted me at high barricades with simple warnings. To all of them I am in debt.

I have always believed that life is a never-finished finishing school. I have not become all I once wanted to be. This collection of small moments proves I am still under construction. This book holds the blueprints of some old visions laid by, the maps of the half-walked alleys I never should have gone down. These events are the dream pieces of old erector sets, which with careful reading can be reassembled. Sure, there are parts missing and packing lists improperly itemized. So don't read this book to see how to do anything. Just sit with me and wonder at how closely our pilgrimages have passed. I have the feeling our journeys have been similar. But even if they are not, true pilgrims still understand each other. All pilgrims know that you don't go on pilgrimages seeking life. The pilgrimage *is* life.

Calvin Miller
Ft. Worth, Texas
1997

I. From the Manufacturer

I. From the Manufacturer

I Made This Product

I Guarantee This Product

FROM THE MANUFACTURER

THERE ARE NO MANUALS FOR IDENTIFYING or assembling the soul. We never complete the work of becoming mature nor even of fitting life's pieces perfectly together. This is the best of all merely human beatitudes: Blessed are all of those who understand that life is always under construction, for such are able to amend the blueprints even as they dream up the changes. We, the unfinished, always manage to admit to our critics, "Please be patient, God is not through with me yet."

All life comes with the instructions "To Be Assembled." To help with the work of putting life together, God has given us a lot of how-tos in the Bible. But even more than a construction manual, the Bible contains the shipping manifest of all the parts as we assemble our maturity day by day. The directions for assembly are lifelong and complex. To define ourselves in the best possible way, we must pursue Christlikeness.

The great battles of life are mostly inward. It is inside ourselves that we war over issues of origin and destiny.

Are these wars won or lost? It is rarely possible to exorcise the demons that lobby for our insignificance unless we are convinced that we have come from and are headed toward God.

There is a certain tidiness in not having a creator. There is no moral obligation. There is no need to look upward to thank anyone. Daily bread is not a matter of divine providence but of our sweating it out. Praying is unnecessary since security does not reside in the heavens but in our own keeping. When we have no maker, there is no need to have an owner's manual for the soul.

Those who jettison faith in the Almighty all too often believe they are in charge of their world. The claims of the self-made come clad in ego. Arrogance often radiates from the blatantly Godless. Those who kill Jehovah, find it is awfully hard to keep from taking his place. Once you say out loud, "I have no maker," the next line is often, "So here are my doctrines, and this is my throne. Who shall contest me?" With no one in the sky to humbly thank, it is customary for the mere mortal achiever to take cosmic credit.

In 1962 when John Glenn orbited the earth, we Americans were very impressed with the event. We were rather in awe of Glenn's achievement, but we were even more in awe of a God who could make a universe predictable enough to permit the wonder.

When the Russian cosmonaut Yuri Gagarin orbited, he became very animated as he flew from day to night in 90-minute earth-laps. In his excitement he shouted out, "I am an eagle! I am an eagle!" This was offensive to many of us Americans. Perhaps we were offended by Gagarin because we like to see at least a shred of humility in our heroes.

In contrast to our opinions about Yuri Gagarin's swaggering boast, most of us have stood in awe of Stephen Hawking. Defying overwhelming physical challenges, he has drawn an immense portrait of the universe for us. We feel as though his picture holds a fascination that would not be there if we were alone in the universe. Whether he is willing to acknowledge it or not, the portrait that Hawking has painted points to something beyond the physical.

Perhaps God knew that down here on earth things get a little tangled, and most of those who debate God's existence lead comfortable lives. Well-fed atheists can get pushy with their blasé negativism. Materialism and nihilism sleep well together. Secular philosophers debate life best at full tables.

But God comes to those who are lonely: to those who cry out from empty tables he whispers above their crying, "Weep not. There is meaning in abundance. I have made you, and I have made this world. Peace is all around you for the taking. I guarantee the product. My word is my warranty." You may count on the wisdom of Julian of Norwich: "All shall be well and all shall be well and all manner of things shall be well."

The emotionally bereft must leave all debates about God and his existence to the atheists. This small manual for the unfinished soul is for those who readily admit their need for God. I am readily a part of those who are needy.

God is the maker of our lives, and he guarantees his unfailing presence, his grace, his forgiveness, and his peace. This book is dedicated to the completion of our unfinished souls. The finishing is God's work. The faith that he will do it, ours.

THE BRAIN

*Minds and brains are not the same thing. All of us
know plenty of people who have the latter but not the
former. The brain is the vehicle of our obedience, the
mind is the driver. These fourteen lines came to me after
an encounter with a verse of Scripture: "Let this mind
be in you which was also in Christ Jesus."—May 1976*

Gray-wrinkled, three-pound thing, I clearly see
I cannot trap you with an EEG.
You nervy organ, you! Skull-cased but free—
A brazen challenge to psychiatry.
Soft mass, I cannot help resenting you
Each time they search and probe for my I.Q.
Half of Einstein's lobe was twice of you,
You joyless megavolt, computer shoe.

Be careful, Judas organ, or you'll find
God cauterizes every rebel mind.
You small gray lump, you always seethe and grind,
Spend small electric currents thinking blind.

Yet you're the only shabby place I see
That His great mind may come to dwell in me.

PENTEUCHIO

Some years ago in reading one of my favorite theologians, I was struck with his concept of the burden of God. When God created human beings and set them on the earth with the gift of free will, he endowed his creatures with the ultimate power to reject even himself, the very God who had fashioned them in the first place. This allegory is a retelling of an old Italian tale. It resulted from my own reckoning with the burden of God.

In a small hamlet of Germany, as the sixteenth century was pouring through the hour-glass, there lived an aging, childless rabbi named Japheth ben Levi. One Thursday, as he was sitting in his old wicker chair and reading the Pentateuch, he began to weep. He pulled his prayer shawl far forward over his face and waited for the tears to stop. He did not believe that as a general rule prayer should be offered while one cried, for he felt that God had enough problems trying to keep the complaining world happy. It was not kind to add to God's burdens.

But alas, his tears would not stop. His prayers were choked by his sobs. "I am sorry to come to you crying as so much of the world customarily does, but my grievance is too long for a letter and too heavy to wait any longer. God, I must ask you this: Is it right that you should have made yourself a whole world of children and that my wife, Esther, and I should be condemned to live alone? Your children are as the sands of the sea, but we have no inheritance at all. Furthermore, your family is not well behaved.

While I hate to point this out to you, many of your children are giving you a bad name, what with being murderers and malcontents and loud-mouthed politicians. If you will give us a son, I promise you that my boy will turn out no worse than some of yours have." Japheth felt as though he was being sassy to God, but it was, after all, little more than he really felt.

God listened to the rabbi's complaints. He didn't mind his weeping, it was just that God, like any father, loved his children. He resented Japheth's picking out a few bad apples and coming down so hard on his whole family. He was tempted to put Japheth's request in the "to be answered" file. But the rabbi's tears had so affected heaven that the angels began loitering around the weeping rabbi and crying themselves.

"Why talk to me, Japheth?" said God, at last. "If you think my family has too many brigands and cutthroats, consider that I have also created an ungrateful rabbi or two."

Things get quiet in heaven when God gets loud. After a long silence, God spoke again: "Japheth, you have a father but no son, am I right?"

"You are right, God! You are always right!" agreed the rabbi.

"Then you know the work of being a child, am I right?"

"You are right, of course, God. You are always right!"

"But you do not know the really hard work of being a father. Am I right?"

"Yes, God, always and ever you are right, which I might add makes your work easier than mine!"

"Do not sass me, Japheth. I am going to give you offspring."

"But how can this be? I am old, and Esther is as barren as a desert."

"Do you have a table leg?"

"Yes, I do, God. You know I do. I have four table legs; they are on our table, keeping it far enough from the floor to lift our simple meals."

"Well, take one leg off your table and whittle out a marionette."

"But, God, if I take a leg off the table, it will teeter and be unstable."

"So, Japheth, do you think that any real miracles can occur when the whole world is stable? Why should people be allowed to set at stable tables while all heaven is in an uproar? Do you want a son or not?"

"To be sure."

"And one thing more."

"Yes, God."

"Always carve with the grain. Making children can get ugly if you botch the creative process. If the knife slips on a cross-grain, you could gouge an ugly scar into your offspring. Make a scarred face or two and people will blame me. They will say, 'There must not be a God, or Japheth's little one would not be born so ugly and scarred.' This I can tell you, Japheth: when you create children, you put your whole reputation on the line. Make ugly children and you're sure to take a lot of heat."

As soon as God got through talking to the rabbi, the sky was shattered by lightning. The rabbi didn't mind this too much since he saw lightning bolts as nothing more than God's exclamation points. The lightning was a dramatic place for God to quit talking. He did. And that was about all that happened on that Thursday.

"What are you doing to my table?" demanded Esther on Friday morning upon entering the kitchen.

"Why talk to me, Esther? I am only obeying the

Almighty," said the rabbi as he continued sawing.

"So God doesn't like this table either. I told you it was ugly when we bought it."

"Esther, I have some wonderful news. God wants me to carve out a marionette, which in time will become our son."

"Why would God give us a son when his own children behave so badly?"

"I mentioned that to him. He said parenting is harder work than we imagine."

"Well, if you're going to carve, be sure you carve with the grain. No use creating unnecessary birth defects."

"Funny, but that's what he said!"

"Who?"

"God."

The table leg was suddenly sawed through. It fell to the floor and hit the rabbi's foot.

"Oww, God!" yelled Japheth as he turned his eyes to the ceiling and began holding his injured foot while he hopped around the room on the other. "That hurt, God," he yelled to the ceiling.

"Why talk to me, Japheth? Do you think you can bring children into the world without pain?" asked God.

Japheth said nothing else. He sat down almost immediately and began to carve. "What shall I call you, little one?" he said to the still unshaped table leg. "I know. Since I first complained of my childlessness while reading the Pentateuch, I shall call you *Penteuchio.*"

In so simple a way was the table leg given a name, and the name stuck.

As the rabbi carved, he would talk to the table leg, and day by day it looked less and less like a table leg and more and more like a marionette.

By the fourth week the rabbi was carving down past the

marionette's eyes, and as he did, the eyes snapped suddenly alive. They darted around the room, as though they were looking for what mischief they might cause. This so unnerved the old rabbi that he tied an old sock around Penteuchio's eyes so that his skitterish glances were hidden from the craftsman. With the eyes covered, Japheth continued his work and by the sixth week had carved down past the head, setting the chin free at last to move.

"How goes life, old man?" said Penteuchio.

"I am your father. Show me some respect. You will not speak to me in such a manner! Do you hear me, young man?"

"I'll call you what I please," said the insolent marionette.

Japheth found another old sock and stuck it in the sassy mouth.

"Mffft!" said Penteuchio, trying to talk with the sock wedged between his wooden lips. Once the marionette quit trying to talk, Japheth faced a quandary. Should he go on with this desperate dream or throw his partly formed son in the fireplace?

As his inner battle raged, the rabbi turned to God. "God, should I go on with this or not? It seems Penteuchio may turn out badly."

"This is the burden of all makers, my child. Who can say how a sock-in-the-mouth boy will turn out? When I first made my boy, Adam, I should have put a sock in his mouth. You know what the book says, Japheth: I gave him a thousand orchards, and he picked the only tree I told him he couldn't have. You need to think this over. Keep the sock in the marionette's mouth. Put the table leg in the corner. Fix yourself a bagel, and have a talk with Esther about family planning before you go any further."

So Japheth put Penteuchio in a bag and set him in the

corner. "Should we go on with this, or not?" he asked Esther. "I have reason to believe our little Penteuchio will know more of sin than salvation. He is not even made, and yet he is sassy and sour!"

"A table leg can become either a boy or a brat. It was you who wanted an heir and a son. Now on the brink of having one, would you throw the whole thing in the fire? Perhaps as you carve, you should make sure the sawdust is out of his ears. Then even as you whittle you can teach him the Torah. Maybe the Word of the Lord will clean up his speech. Remember, whittle with the grain."

When Esther was gone, Japheth began working again. His carving was complicated by the old sock over the marionette's eyes and the one in his mouth. He made sure all the sawdust was out of his ears, however. "Now, my little friend, I am going to teach you the Torah, whether you like it or not. 'In the beginning God created the heavens and the earth. . . .' "

So on into the future weeks, the rabbi carved and quoted Scripture. At week ten, when the marionette's arms came free, one of the arms lashed out, grabbed a carving knife, and jammed it in Japheth's leg. The rabbi impulsively cried out, "Oww!" Then he grabbed up an old sock and lashed it around the doll's arms and tied it tightly behind his back.

"Japheth," said God, laughing, "how can one little boy have so many socks and no feet as yet? Your boy isn't turning out so well, is he?"

"Why talk to me, God? Do you think Ghenghis Khan or Nero or Nebuchadnezzar was any better? Believe me, the world swelters under this ungodly family tree of yours, so leave my family alone."

It amazed the rabbi that he was already so defensive about his little one, when his own boy was not even finished. Old Japheth knew he was falling in love with the boy. He found it increasingly hard to listen even to the criticism of God. There was nothing to do but to pick up the half-formed child and continue on. It was getting harder and harder to carve around all the socks, but he never gave up trying, and it was impossible to give up hoping.

In a few days the rabbi had quoted all of Genesis and Exodus to his blind and gagged offspring.

"Now, young man, we are down to the Levitical code. I'm going to keep carving while you learn the whole book of law. Remember it is only a short few years till your bar mitzvah, and oaken or not you're going to stand up there with the rest of the scholars and answer the questions." And so as he sat in his little wicker chair, he carved and quoted, and quoted and carved.

As long as Japheth kept Penteuchio's arms tied securely down, the work went well. By the fifteenth week the marionette was complete. Suddenly Penteuchio lashed out with his little oak legs, kicking his maker again and again. It was only with great difficulty that the rabbi managed to lash the thrashing legs together with yet another sock. After the legs were tightly cinched, Japheth put Penteuchio down and set a huge, heavy stone on him.

Then he looked down at him and began to weep. "Ah, my little son! How much I should like to take all your binding away and set you free. But I am afraid you would do me much mischief."

"Mffft . . . mffft," said Penteuchio, strangling to reply to the musings of the rabbi. It broke the old man's heart to see Penteuchio wedged under the huge stone. Japheth blew out the lamp and left his wooden son orphaned in the darkness.

"Esther," said the old man, entering their bedroom, "our

21

boy is done. He's under a huge stone, bound and gagged. I haven't the slightest hope that upon liberating him he will do us honor."

"Well, you can't keep him planted under rocks for the rest of his life, Japheth."

"I know, Esther. In the morning, I'll consider what to do about him."

Esther slept poorly and Japheth not at all. At three in the morning, he could hear a strange thumping coming from the workshop. He got up and went downstairs. Penteuchio had managed to kick free of the sock that bound his legs together. Japheth found it and worked at getting the fetter back in place. The marionette kept kicking at Japheth's arms as the rabbi worked at retying his legs together. Finally Penteuchio was once again bound and gagged and beneath the stone. The rabbi sat down at the table once more. He heard a familiar voice.

"Japheth, this is God. . . ."

"I know. . . ."

"You've got to let him go, you know."

"But what if he disowns me and embarrasses me or makes me cry for sheer size of his disobedience? What will I do then?"

"So you're asking me, Japheth, are you? I had a daughter—my first daughter—who ran off with a snake and then gave birth to a murderer. I tell you, it's much easier to make children than to set them free. But you can't create them to be free and then tie them up with socks and keep them under rocks. I didn't do that to Adam, and I didn't do that to you. So, Japheth, now you know the burden of God, do you not?"

God got quiet, and old Japheth sat for two hours wrangling over what it meant to love an unlovely little creature.

There was no question about it, he did love little Penteuchio. With everything in him, the rabbi desired to set the boy free. With all his strength, Japheth stood up and walked across the room and lifted the lid on the box. He took the stone off his little one. Then he took away the sock that covered his eyes. Those strange little eyes squinted their wooden lids to adjust to the light. His eyes were now free to look, and his little wooden ears were free to hear, and so the old man spoke. "Tell me this, my little one: if I take the gag out of your mouth, will you speak honorably?"

The marionette nodded in assent.

The gag was removed.

"Oh, Father . . . ," said the boy. The very word brought tears of joy to the soul of old Japheth. "I love you. Please take the socks from my arms and I will embrace you."

Japheth, having waited all his life for such an embrace, quickly complied. The sock came off. The boy's thin oak arms shot upward and fell around the thick neck of his maker and father.

"Oh, Father. If you but take the cords from my legs, I will walk with you to synagogue."

Japheth's clumsy but kind hands took off the sock that bound the legs of his little one. The boy leapt from his lap and danced about the room singing, "I'm free! I'm free! I am forever free!" His delight was so great that the old man took his little wooden fingers in his own and the two of them danced around the room.

The old man's merriment was short lived. In but a moment, the boy shook free of his grasp and ran toward the low-burning embers of the fireplace. He reached into the fire and grabbed a burning log and tossed it into the kindling box. There were flames everywhere! While the old man worked at getting the fire under control, Penteuchio jumped up into the rabbi's wicker chair, then leapt out of the nearby window and hurried off into the night. The house was saved, but the old artist's little wooden boy was lost. Japheth wept and resigned himself to childlessness.

Then, and in later years, the rabbi talked often with God, and the two of them often compared stories of their disappointment with their children. In his latter years, Penteuchio widely denied that Japheth had ever been his father. Japheth wept when he thought of the long months that he had labored to bring Penteuchio into the world. He had lived longer than broken-hearted men should have to live. During his final year of life, he said to God, "You told me to set him free, and I did. Now this very son I made denies that I ever made him."

"Why talk to me, Japheth? Many of Adam's children treat me with the same denials. But, Japheth, you played my part and learned my burden. You were a good father, and you freed your child. If it hurts, console yourself by remembering you'll soon be home with me. Heaven is a grand place for fathers to reminisce."

Three hundred years have passed since Japheth was laid to rest in a little German cemetery. But those who live in the villages nearby say that heaven's highest throne has beside it a small wicker chair. There the great God and a wizened rabbi often sit and talk about the high cost of creating children and setting them free. The joy of that wonderful place has been made wise by pain. Heaven's truths have all been proved on a blue-white planet where some children steal old men's dreams and others eat fruit that is forbidden.

24

Carbon Chauvinism

On September 6, 1978, upon reading a Carl Sagan interview in which he insisted that all life was carbon based.

Today Carl Sagan proclaimed his conjecture—
A brilliant and forceful, instructional lecture—
And we were astounded insane.
Who can deny it?
A methane prism may surely contain
Divergent life-forms, carbon-based like our own.
The schism between their form-similarity
And our earthly graces does not harmonize.
To find two-armed beings with ventral sweet faces
Just won't occur in other remote evolutions.

What then, my dear humanoids? What shall we say
To our purple-finned, multi-green tentacled brothers?
"You, our dear carbon-based, sweet bluish blobs,
Are family to us, we carbon-based snobs.
Carbon composes all star-slimy sod—
To carbon we sing—we offer our laud.
For carbon is life, and carbon is God."

Yuri Gagarin, Self-Proclaimed Atheist Eagle

Written in reaction to Gagarin's overevaluation of his shallow-orbit triumph.

Astro—Arragants
Anodized in hooded glass
Peeking out through bubbled visors.
Silver-suited aerialists,
Asbestos wrapped like pudgy tourists,
Clicking bulky cameras
In mittens of aluminum
Floating where the cows of yesterday
Jumped over the Sea of Tranquility.

High flying, silver showoffs playing golf,
Clothed only in an inch of atmosphere,
Calling, "God, where are you?"

Surprised they were to find God home.
While they were out moon-gadding.
"Come in, you shallow orbiters.
Have you forgotten that I tracked these voids
Before your flimsy rockets wobbled on their concrete
    springs?
I've been here waiting all these centuries.
To meet you in this lunar closet of my galaxied
    estate . . .

Bragging of your half-block triumph
In a galaxy a hundred-trillion light years wide.
Try Vega next time,
Or get thee to a gunnery
And fire at me from Mars."

And then the parachute billowed
And the eagle landed in Siberia.
God was there too.
But he rarely makes his presence known
Where the glaciers crowd the green seas
And the ice is far too cold for truth.

FIAT LUX

*To Stephen Hawking, in appreciation for his views on
the unfolding universe as expressed in* A Brief History
of Time.

Fiat lux: Let there be optic nerves!
Fiat caelum! Let there be the skies!
Let there be spinal cords which serve
To make discovery the task of mortal eyes.
If vision had come first, then sight,
We could have stared for ages into black,
And waited for that splintering of night
That shivered chaos with a silver track.

Oh, God, why did you trim the universe
With light before you made humanity,
Waiting out your million-decade curse
In dark omnipotence so casually?

   You were unplugged, low-wattage Trinity,
   Night blinded, windowless divinity.

Two

I have two old friends who, after forty years of marriage to other mates, learned to spell hope in the simple syllable of a second chance.

I wondered how each had found the other.
  They were two whose togetherness with other loves
  had shared other children, other laughter,
  other pain in separate worlds.
  Each had watched their first beloved
  strangled in the tentacles of melanoma.
  Each had buried hope in gagging
  grief and blaring silence.
Each had walked that long, long way
from hearse to grave and back again.
  Each had stared into the dark of empty bedrooms
  and felt the hot tears slash an older, wiser face.
  Each had learned to set the table for one—
  that staring-straight-ahead obscenity—
  one plate, one fork, one crystal glass
  that didn't mind a thumbprint
  when there was no one there to see it.
They remembered how they both felt
the cold seep up from the chilled, unheated earth
around the new sod graves of their first loves.
Brutality was now the cruel instruction of their choice.

Years ago they had picked other mates.
They chose as young lovers always choose—
mates to flatter all their self-importance when others said,
   "Isn't he handsome?"
   "Isn't she beautiful?"
   "And wasn't he a catch, with his degrees and income?"
   "And isn't she just right? Her father was the mayor,
      you know!"
And so they dated most conspicuously.
Their engagement photograph in all the papers,
making all who knew them near-neurotics
lest their wedding gifts prove not *quite right*
for such a *just right* pair.

Flattered by their youth,
these separate lovers picked their first low-mortgage house.
It was not the house they hoped to own
when they would later keep up with the Joneses.
   It was just a house that they could occupy until they
      saved the
   money that would buy their noble dream.
   But age makes older lovers wise,
   And from the back side of the hearse
   each lost a love and found the truth.
They were captive in those younger years
to all the world wanted them to be:
and they were perfect, and felt perfect
Before life taught them crying.

   The years had weathered their complexions:
   too red at last for makeup,
      too blemished for photographers to hide.
Their children taught them crying

30

and brought them far too much embarrassment
to keep their perfect public reputations.
And thus they learned a need for God
they only said they knew before.
    And they grew real, yes, real, and yet again more real.

Then at last the growing melanoma came.
    They fought the deep and hidden monster
    with huge machines that rumbled radiation.
    And each day's loss reminded them
    that light is not forever and the eye at last
    will be as hollow as the night.
    And when the light is gone,
    it is far too dark to expect the world to stop and say,
    "Aren't they wise? Aren't they knowing?
    Let us learn from them
    as special teaching friends."

But wisdom moves so slow sometimes,
when grief has amputated hope with darkness
and crept upward from the numb and icy turf
cut like an earthen wound in winter snow.
They had buried their own hearts,
interred their will to live.

But God does not allow his grace to slumber long.
    There came to each a second Easter for their grief.
    The tomb gave up its hopelessness.
    The sealing stone rolled back, light shot through granite.
    Then the day of visitation came.
    Angels woke them both
    on an empty Saturday, somewhere near an ordinary
        market.

They met at last.
Each was dead of heart, dead of hope, alone.
Her without him.
Him without her.

"We haven't long to hold the light," he said.
"We haven't long," she said as she extended her hand,
swollen with heavy knuckles that seemed unlovely
    even as she reached.
"She's gone; would she have minded?" he asked himself.
"Him, too. Would he have cared?" she wondered.
They touched again.
Old hands do not play at passion.
Eros is the cheap and hurried need of youth.
    Their love was truly chaste now, too studied for
        impulsiveness,
    too knowing for rash need.
"I'll make you a salad," she said,
ashamed her overtures for love were all so practical.
"My irises are in the second year," he said.
He, too, could think of only small beginnings.

And, for the first time in heavy scores of months,
two sets of footprints scrubbed the dewy grass
because the years did not allow them
to lift aging feet as high as they would like.
    Those double footprints moved in one direction
    across the city park
    to the stoop of an old house still young enough to
        live a little while.
    And sure enough,
    the irises were all about the porch,
        and inside, the silent lovers ate a crisp, fresh salad.

Their loneliness at last condensed itself into four slippers
set to dry upon a concrete stoop
that waited while naked feet
thrilled to feel the wet grass growing all about the irises.

The banners of their castle
waved proudly from a swagging laundry line—
    one frayed and faded flannel shirt
    and one bright gingham dress.
    They wore them ever after—even on Memorial Day,
    when they attended memories of other bargains
    made with former lovers
    in the springtime of their lives,
    when their backs were straighter,
    but their hearts were not made wise.

TO MIFFY THOMAS

*A child friend of mine left before I could kiss her
good-bye. After she left us, I waited through a long first
day to let my grief gather wit. Then on the following
day, her second day in heaven, I wrote this eulogy.
—January 5, 1981*

I've waited till your second day. I knew
Your first day there would seem to you a treat.
You'd gaze about in wonder at the view
Of all that city gathered in one street.
So many I know here are quite afraid
To face their final fears and cross the sea.
You swam so easily! What courage made
You unafraid to walk eternity?

Did God appear a high-rise trinity?
Did glass or tow'ring crystal dazzle you?
Did he not cry, "Let this child come to me
And give her room to skip this avenue!"

At those grand gates which close against the night,
He scooped you up and carried you to light.

THE GIFT OF ZEBEDEE

We have no record of how Zebedee felt when his sons
went to follow Jesus. I wonder if he felt abandoned.

The surging sound of salted sea,
that singing, sparkling, swelling sigh,
the scream of gulls against the sky:
these are the sounds of Galilee.

Bronze fishers bent by years of debt,
all moving slowly, silent, free,
sea-lashed in lonely agony,
by mocking hemp and broken nets.

At once, yet independently,
the old man works so slowly now,
the light of God upon his brow,
this patriarch called Zebedee.

A stranger, shadow first, intrudes,
Throws out his arms above the flow
and shouts across the blue tableau;
he calls, divides, demands, precludes.

And now the old man sits alone;
a voice has called above the sea
to take the sons of Zebedee.
His sons are gone. His sons are gone.

Old men are orphaned by a whim—
Messiah's come to claim the day,
and children up and walk away.
Yes, Zebedee, they've followed him.

"I'm down here, God of froth and foam!
My leathered hands are on the oars!
I'll pull the wood and reach for shore
and conquer Galilee . . . alone."

II. Reading the Directions

II. Reading the Directions

Reading the Directions

If there is a single book which may justly be called an owner's manual for the unfinished soul, it is the Bible. The Bible is *the book*—the archetype by which all other books must be measured. It is God's one-volume reply to every category of human hurt and need.

If there is a single book that stands for Western culture, it must be the Bible. George Bernard Shaw once said that English is the language of Shakespeare, Milton, and the Bible. The Bible contains the ethics of the Ten Commandments, the reverence of the Lord's Prayer, the holistic philosophy of the Beatitudes, and the ageless parables of Christ.

In this one volume are the poems of David, the commandments of Moses, the tender romance of Ruth, the plaintive dirges of Jeremiah. Here in ordinary ink, on ordinary paper, are the tales of ordinary believers whose extraordinary faith undergirds the development of the West. Around the Bible gather the naïve, the informed, the cruel, the compassionate. All of them claim that in the Bible they have found a specific foundation for their way of life. The Bible is so simple that children can read it, and yet theologians stand dumb before its profundity.

Only the grandeur of Scripture can explain our utter need and undying fascination with it. Those needs must be explained in simple ways that interpret life and serve the important truths of scholars as well as needy children. I, for one, am a dependent believer. I need to read the Book of Life's directions regularly. As I read, I find my place in the world, and I hear from my Maker. In reading the Bible I make life livable, one word at a time.

THE BOOK

This was written in protest of those biblical scholars who know their instruments of surgery, but have rarely spoken to their patient.

The Book! The Book!
It was, and is,
And will be evermore.
Born in realms removed,
Old as uncooled moons,
Yet young in every age.
Emanating from the center of the middle—
The pulp and fiber of all being.
God's word it is,
In starry volumes
For galaxied eternities,
Yet falling on us gently,
One letter at a time.
Near print on near paper—
Whispered messages in ink—
From our upward, longing lover.

Distant words from other worlds?
Never.
Words born here in history,
Close enough for us to touch,
Yet hatched
In languageless infinity.
God comes to us in star tracks,

Wearing syllables of gossamer,
That leap from new-formed clay.
God, clothed
In papyrus and codex,
Flying over oriental fields
In whispered wind and printed spirit.

Sing! God has a stylus in his hands.
He shouts in quill and ink,
"Here I am
Within this Book
This Book of books,
This word incomparable,
This vellum currency
Surpassing excellence—
This scroll majestic.
Here is my majesty
In common nouns and verbs,
I gave to babes and warlords,
To Aramaic shepherds,
And Hittite vagabonds,
To Hebrew, Greek, and Latin monks,
To Elizabethan scholars,
And, last of all, to you.

"In this Book I come
Whispering in ink,
Breathing,
Revealing,
Disclosing,
Never quitting!
All bright, determined,
My aching silence shouts,

'I have a Son.
My once begotten
Rises ever upward
Above the center of my Shaddai papyrus.' "

His word is living ink.
Hold it to your ear
Like the conch of YHWH,
And you will hear the Red Sea roar—
The rattle of iron rims on cobble stones—
The neighing of war horses—
The soft tread of camels in the sand,
The snap of breaking loaves,
The clear, clean song of leper choirs
Singing in the streets.

Listen to the warm!
Almighty love is
Resonating through the Pentateuch,
Swelling in the histories,
Bursting symphonically
In psalms of timpani
And flutes above the misty seas.
Can you hear
These thrumming cadences,
These brassy fanfares of the Easter news?

Our God *can* write!
He lifts his starry quill,
And the ages beg for parchment.
A thousand pages
Of Adam's sad biography,
And on each one

The grace-drawn portrait
Of his Son.
His words, wide as Andromeda,
Stir the artist to create,
The compassionate to care,
The disconsolate to laughter,
The mute to oratorios,
The paralytics to fervent dancing.

The word, the word!
The singing distant word!
Jehovah with a pen nib dipped in such fire
As warms the grave
With the hot ink of heaven's tears.
Such a weeping God
Will use his own tears
To quench the fires of hell.
His is the present poetry of suffering,
The promised prose of hope,
Settling on us
Like a sparrow,
Small and inobtrusive
Like a dove,
Pure in its intent
Like an eagle,
Visible and powerful.

His Book is ours—
A light-year lithograph
Printed in
a thousand etchings
Of the never-fading face of God—
Burning through our weak morality

Like a new-born sun
Ordered into sky—
Circling the earth
And orbiting our private world in light.

THE HOLY BIBLE—PCV
(POLITICALLY CORRECT VERSION)

This version, based on a portion of the Gospel of John, is really a plea for biblical simplicity.

JOHN 7:53   And everyone, both minorities and social determiners, went to his or her own house in the typically sociostructured city of Jerusalem.

JOHN 8:1   But Jesus went up to the Mount of Olives. He did not do this to try to be "above" others socioeconomically, but because the population density on the mountain was less environmentally confining, affording him a more meditative matrix for ego integration.

JOHN 8:2   Now, early in the morning—but still well within the hours of fair employment practices—Jesus came again to the temple of Jehovah. (He did not use the name Jehovah to express his Jewishness in an arrogant religious exclusivism that would condemn others who speak of the universal Spirit using equally meaningful names.) And he sat down and taught them.

JOHN 8:3   Then certain religious potentates of the

masculine-structured society brought him an oppressed member of the gender-challenged who had been caught in the act of her sexually indiscriminate employment. As an act of religious brutality, she was shoved to Jesus' feet without any bodily covering, in a state of enforced fabric denial.

JOHN 8:4   They said to him, "Rabbi, this psychosexual, gender-oppressed person was caught performing her deviant, but preferential, lifestyle employment."

JOHN 8:5   "Now Moses, our D.S.S.M. (Dead Semitic Sinaitic Male) leader, said in the coercive Torah compulsories that spun off the Ten Behavioral Restrictives that she should be stoned. What do you say?"

JOHN 8:6   This they said to him, apparently overstressing him with interrogatives. They waited to prove him guilty of doctrinal aberrations. They wanted to label him with sexual discrimination. They wanted to display his unfair tendency to look down on people with sexual and ethical lifestyle differences. Then they would be able to bring their own personal, critical, male establishmentarianisms fully against his differing prejudices. But Jesus stooped down and wrote on the ground with his finger. They found it somewhat refreshing that he did not use his finger to point at them

47

in sociocommunal separation. Yet they found it altogether baffling that he wrote his message in the soft earth. We are not told what the message was.

JOHN 8:7 But when they continued asking him, he raised himself up, not to indicate his feelings of class superiority, but merely to be better heard, and said, "Let him or her who is without socially conditioned prejudices among you, first cast a stone at this person." He knew that, reprehensible or not, most people had committed acts of socially conditioned prejudice.

JOHN 8:8 Again he stooped down and wrote on the ground.

JOHN 8:9 Then those who heard this person speak were convicted by their own occasional lapses into acts resulting from bad moral conditioning. They began to slip quietly away as though suddenly remembering specific resultant acts of this unacceptable conditioning. The oldest left first, since they had more backlog of such moral strictures. They appeared to be guilty, though none of them would have used that word to describe it: the word *guilty* was out of vogue.

JOHN 8:10 Finally they were all gone, and Jesus said to the gender-oppressed woman, "Gender-

Oppressed Person, where are your accusers? Have none of the male-dominated religious establishment been able to quell their self-repression long enough to stone you?"

JOHN 8:11   "No one, Lord!" she said, wishing she would not have used the word *Lord*. (She meant it not as a terrible prefeudal term of masculine empowerment. It was just how she felt at the time.)

But Jesus said to her, "Neither do I condemn you. Go, but beware of going right back into your preferential lifestyle. It's not just that your occupation is somewhat unacceptable to others: this kind of thing can be damaging to your own sense of ego integration."

SCRIPTURE MAN

We all react to hypocrites. Their hang-ups make us wonder about the worthiness of religion.

Lois Schwarz had been married to Clark Schwarz for two years before she began to suspect that Clark was really *Scripture Man.* One Thursday night she found a pair of blue leotards in the clothes hamper.

"Yours?" she asked Clark.

"Uh huh," he confessed, looking down.

"Clark . . ." She paused. "Can you leap tall steeples in a single bound? Are you faster than a speeding Lear jet full of cable evangelists?"

Yes. It was all true.

"Honey, since you know, would you promise not to tell a soul? And maybe you could help me wash my costume here at home. Remember, don't put the red tights with the blue leotards." He blushed.

That's how Lois found out. At first she felt proud that her husband was Scripture Man. She thrilled just knowing that he could run into the smallest church, throw off his Dockers and tweedy coat, and be Scripture Man. Only his Oakwood High class ring (which no one ever seemed to notice) told the truth about him: he was simply Clark Schwarz.

Still, Scripture Man never missed a chance to help anyone. When a couple was about to get a divorce, he would crash through their front window and hand them a card that said "Divorce not, but grow in grace." On the back of such cards always appeared a list of relevant Bible verses. If a man was about to cheat on his income tax, Scripture Man would crash through the ceiling at just the right moment with a card that said "Cheat not, for the soul that cheateth shall die." On the back of the card, to be sure, was a well-researched index of Scripture verses forbidding dishonesty.

At first, Lois felt good helping launder his costumes and keeping his cards ready, but before long she felt uneasy about Clark. What caused her dismay? Well, Clark had started wearing his costume around the house and was becoming a little wearisome. One afternoon when she was veging out before the *Sally Jessy Raphael* show, he gave her a card that said "Watch not, lest thine eyes corrupt thee." And one Tuesday night after finding out that she had given a plastic-container party for her friends, he gave her another card which read "Tupperware not, thou whited sepulcher." Bit by bit, Lois began to grow weary.

As Clark became more and more self-righteous, he began to snag his leotards trying to leap Episcopal spires. Before long he found he could scarcely leap Pentecostal churches. Finally his leotards were so full of snags that his ministry began to lose ground in public opinion polls.

One night, while he was off on a flight to rebuke a Baptist with a "Dance not" card and an Episcopalian with a "Gamble not" card, Lois couldn't stand it anymore: she called the *New York Times* and blew Clark's cover. He was furious with Lois. "How could you?" he screamed at her.

She handed him a small card. "Fume not," it read, "rather love your wife so that when your days on earth are over you may be received into eternal habitations." There were a lot of Scripture references on the back of the card.

SUPER SEMANTICS

I hate big words, so I rebuke them every chance I get.

At last we've acquired some sophistication;
We're an erudite and intelligent nation.
And now to speak simply without complication
Is the basest and lowest humiliation.

So what was bad breath is now *halitosis;*
And what was heart failure is now a *thrombosis;*
A quirk of the mind is now a *psychosis;*
And hardening veins, *arteriosclerosis.*

Civil defiance is now called a *coup;*
We eat *minestrone* we used to call stew;
We don't send out men, we *deploy a crew;*
And *low spectral frequency* once was called blue.

A general now is a *war strategist;*
And a private eye is a *crime analyst.*
Atmospheric pollution was once smoke and mist
In our simplified, long-ago, glossary list.

But all words and phrases are now more austere:
Even the trash man is a *grand engineer.*
Yet nowhere is all this new language more queer
Than that used in churches by churchmen, I fear.

Hermeneutics becomes the term new and sweet;
And the student of Scripture is an *exegete;*
For discussion, the term is *dialogue* now;
And knowing someone is defined *I and Thou.*

Psalm twenty-three now reads something like this:
"The Lord is my internal-external bliss.
In agrarian areas there I shall lie,
Nonturbulent reservoirs flowing nearby.

"Though I walk through the valley of shadow and death,
My need disposition and libido rest.
I am not neurasthenic or ever depressed;
My cup overflows with abundance possessed.

"If mystical grace and the quality good
Follow my steps as I think that they should,
then by my good deeds and sound eschatology
I'll reach heaven by way of my soteriology."

This all seems to say with great dignity,
That nothing is simple as all used to be.
To cloud understanding and deepen the night
Seems better than firing one candle to light.

III. The Parts List

III. THE PARTS LIST

The Parts List

Heaven's leading department on
the sixth day of creation was *Human Design*. According to
the Psalms, we are fearfully and wonderfully made. *Fearfully* and *wonderfully* are the manufacturer's adverbs. He
assembles us with awe and reverence.

God is a creator whose universal construction was
hushed by the joy of all he created. "My frame was not
hidden from you," says the psalmist, "when I was made in
the secret place. When I was woven together in the depths
of the earth." The book of Job celebrates that same creative
fetal work of God when the writer says, "Your hands
shaped me and made me. . . . Remember that you molded
me like clay. . . . Did you not pour me out like milk and
curdle me like cheese, [and] clothe me with skin and flesh
and knit me together with bones and sinews?"

This is *how* God did it. But the real parts list that counts
is not arms and legs and sinews or any of the tangible
elements of his creation. The real parts that compose our
individuality are things like Ego, Identity, Discipline,

Sexuality, and the Joy of being human.

There are not many working parts on the Manufacturer's parts list. But only when they are all in place does meaningful living become possible. So we can understand why Socrates said that the undisciplined life is not worth living. This was, of course, Jesus' idea also. Those who learn to control their passions and negate their own arrogance will fall heir to workable virtues. They will be able to say, "I have been made by God. Pardon me, for I must stop and celebrate my Manufacturer." When all the working parts are in place, life itself is a wonder.

*The following parable was the result of one of the many
interior bouts I have had with televangelism. So much is
good about religious television, but its excesses leave
me feeling guilty that I sometimes indict the good along
with the bad. To any who use television for evil
purposes, I ask you to read the strange case of Dr.
Oneida and his healing. To those whose ministry is
altogether wholesome, I offer you only blessings.*

Once there was a certain televangelist named Dr. Oneida.
Although he constantly told his millions of viewers that
they should be filled with joy, he often found himself
disconsolate.

"Why are you so depressed?" said Sister Bentley, his
assistant, wagging her long finger at him. *"I* fully trust in
our Lord and am never depressed even when my Paraclete
Platinum hair rinse is darkening at the roots."

"Well," sighed her boss, "my old jet airplane has only
two engines and seats only ten people. You know, Sister
Bentley, that the plane is not large enough to take our ever-
growing crusade team to various cities of the world."

"Well then, I suggest that you pray for a new vision. Ask
God to give you the desires of your heart. Just name it and
claim it. It works for me when I'm out shopping for costume jewelry."

So Dr. Oneida prayed, but no vision came. He prayed
even more, still no vision. He even prayed Saturday after
his golf game. Still no vision. So he gave it all up on

Saturday night and ordered a Pizza Supreme with jalapeños and anchovies. At last the vision came.

In the vision he saw a beautiful white dove descending on a new 20-seat plane with four jet engines. In his dream he saw a beautiful woman pilot whose huge white hair was so stiff with hair spray that her coiffure was unruffled by the ear clamps of her headset. Dr. Oneida began to toss and turn in his bed as the jalapeños enraged his euphoria in the middle of the night. Then it seemed he heard a loud voice, like the great beast of the Apocalypse. He could not tell if the voice in the vision was rising from below or descending from above. But the message of the voice was clear: "Go thou and buy this twenty-million-dollar airplane, that thy glory may flow. Thou shalt soar like lightning in the east, like splendor in the west, like fire in Babylon. Thou shalt name thy plane *Dove I,* and it will be the official airplane of the world-wide, miracle crusade ministry team."

Dr. Oneida woke up inflamed with his vision. But his great mood did not last long, for his ministry income was not enough to buy *Dove I.* His listeners were not giving enough to buy the plane. He knew what he must do. He must challenge his viewers to love God more. He must say, "Hasn't God healed your diseases? Hasn't God saved your soul? Hasn't God allowed you to name it and claim it? So why do you not love God more and send him your money in care of my zip code? I'll see that he gets it." At the end of every telecast, he would say, "Dear brothers and sisters, if we do not get more money, our world-wide ministry will be jetless. Jetless! Do you hear me? Jetless and grounded! God has given me a vision of a 900-foot jet plane named *Dove I.* Hallelujah! *Shandallah Lear!* So, please, please, please give to our 'Wings of Glory' offering so that the turbothrust of God's blessing may fall across the runways of the world."

Across the nation, in a small retirement home in Appalachia, there lived a little woman named Sister Felicity who had long been one of the evangelist's supporters. Having grown ill with an incurable illness, she thought to herself, *I must get one of Dr. Oneida's prayer cloths—peradventure God will heal me.*

One night after the evangelist told of his vision, Sister Felicity also had a vision. In her vision she saw herself in heaven. It was a wonderful dream, but it introduced a conflict. When she awoke, she admitted to herself, *While I don't mind being dead, I'm not crazy about dying. Here's what I will do, I will write a letter to Dr. Oneida and this I will say: "Dear Brother Oneida: Here is my life insurance policy. You will notice that I have listed you as the beneficiary. I am not well and probably will not live much longer. All I want in exchange for the policy is one of your wonderful prayer cloths. I'm not quite ready for the Valley of the Shadow yet. Perhaps your cloth will heal me. Here's to the 'Wings of Glory' offering, and may God also give you the turbothrust of his blessing."*

Dr. Oneida received her letter with great joy. He prayed over a prayer cloth and was about to send it to Sister Felicity when he thought to himself, *Sister Felicity believes so wholeheartedly in Christ; if I pray over this prayer cloth, Christ may actually heal her. Then I will never get the proceeds of her life insurance policy, and lo, I will never get my beautiful new Dove I. What then shall I do? Shall I thwart the will of God by healing her? No, a thousand times no! This will I do: I will send her only a grease rag from Action Garage, which will do her little good, and her untimely death will doubtless speed her insurance money to my global ministry.*

When Sister Felicity received the grease rag, she laid it on her frail old body and asked God to heal her in the name of the Father, the Son, the Holy Spirit, and Dr. Oneida. For her rich faith in the first three, God did indeed heal her. "Glory hallelujah! *Shandallah, non-Lear das kaput,*" shouted Sister Felicity in the unknown tongue. She could actually feel Dr. Oneida's prayer cloth healing her body. She wrote to the evangelist reporting the miracle.

"Drats!" said Dr. Oneida as he read of her healing. "Drats!" he said, adding a few noncrusade words. Even as he spoke, the scrawling fingers of a man's hand appeared and wrote some strange words around the center cone of his satellite dish: *Meany, Meany. U takky Parson,* which being interpreted means, "Thou shameful and adulterous televangelist, your kingdom is taken from you. Even your old ten seater will now be taken away, and the turbothrust of my blessings will be given to Sister Ruth on the other network." In a single night, calamity came. His Nielsen ratings fell, and his cable contract was canceled.

After years of poverty and honest living, Dr. Oneida received a postal envelope from Sister Felicity one day. It contained the old grease rag that had so miraculously healed her and a letter:

> Dear Dr. Oneida:
>
> I am returning your prayer cloth. It has worked so well that I am feeling great; I am on a Golden-Age tour of the Holy Land with a group of Sister Ruth's supporters. We climbed the Mount of Olives today—whew!—and bought some olive-wood crosses for everybody in the rest home. If

things are quiet on the West Bank tomorrow, we're all going to be baptized in the Jordan. It sure was too bad that you never got the turbothrust of God's blessing. Sister Ruth has it now, you know. She never had a vision of a dove descending on a new plane, but she did have a vision of a flock of Canada geese flying into the engine of a commercial airliner, so she often travels by Greyhound. I hear your ministry has been hurt. You might try laying this prayer cloth on your financial statements. It worked for me!"

Yours for a better tomorrow,
Sister Felicity

P.S. I saw Sister Bentley. Her hair has gone back to its natural color, and she has quit wearing costume jewelry. Has she lost her faith?

Dr. Oneida wept. He knew it was not Sister Bentley who had turned from the faith. He knew that he was the one who had abandoned God's true vision for his life. He looked at the old grease rag. In spite of his own dishonesty, the grease rag had been Sister Felicity's salvation and his ruin.

"God," he said, "I give you this rag in deep repentance. For it has healed a sick woman and condemned an evil man!"

"Not so," said God, "it has healed you both. It has healed a sick woman of her disease and is now healing an egotist of his pride."

"Is there anything I can ever do to repay your kindness?" asked the evangelist.

"Yes. You will know you are completely healed when you have sent $10 to Sister Ruth on the other network; she needs money for bus tickets, you know."

"You have asked a hard thing, God. To confess our pride is one thing, but to bless our competitors is quite another. Rather, ask me to help in the Adopt-a-Highway program. May I not do this and be clean?"

"You're a slow learner. Must I visit you yet seven times more with boils and scabs?"

Dr. Oneida took ten dollars out of his wallet. He mailed the gift to Sister Ruth, and even as he licked the stamp he knew at last his sin was purged.

When First I Reckoned
with His Love

I first reckoned with God's love in 1945, when I was nine years old. I celebrated the reckoning twenty years later in 1965 with these twenty lines.

"Not my sin, O Lord," I cried,
"That murdered God at Calvary.
Golgotha's Christ was crucified,
But not for my iniquity."

Christ said, "Not so, my son, my son.
For your iniquity,
The lash some forty times save one,
Fell painfully on me.

"Life's lessons come in wood and steel,
And hope is born where vengeance cries.
Forgiveness grows where God must feel
What tears the soul and crucifies.

"Because of your deep guilt and sin
My life was counted loss;
I shuddered in the April wind.
I knew the chafing cross.

"Earth's epoch hourglass spilling time
Has measured centuries since then;
You played your part in cosmic crime.
You need a cosmic friend."

Once upon a time, in a far away land, there lived a king named Olaf and a queen named Bunsie, who was expecting her first child. The last name of this royal family was Sturdley, but the king and queen never used it. The king didn't like last names, and the queen didn't like the sound of *Bunsie Sturdley.*

There was, as is usual in stories like this, a good fairy. She was named Bonnie. Typically for a fairy, Bonnie was good at changing some things into other things, but she was not very good at telling the future. One morning, after she had put on her makeup (good fairies always wear a lot of blush and warm beige base), she went into the throne room to make a prediction to the king and queen.

"Your Majesties!" she began in a loud voice. "I predict that you will have a very lovely child."

It seemed a safe enough prediction, for she did not say whether it would be a boy or girl. She also used the word *lovely,* and that seemed safe, too, for what parents do not think their baby lovely?

The next morning at seven o'clock, the queen had her baby.

"Yee-Gad!" said the doctor when he saw it.

"Is it a boy or a girl?" asked the queen.

"Yes," replied the doctor as he handed the baby to King Olaf.

"Yee-Gad!" the king repeated.

Queen Bunsie could tell by the way everyone said "Yee-Gad!" instead of "How lovely!" that her child must have been less beautiful than she had hoped.

"Olaf, dearie, is it a boy or a girl?" asked Queen Bunsie.

"It's too early to tell!" said the king.

Well, that's how Dru-Ella Sturdley (for they named her after her old uncle Andrew and her old aunt Ella) entered the world. The baby was so ugly that King Olaf made Bonnie, the good fairy, stand in the corner two weeks for false prophecy.

The queen cried for three weeks because Dru-Ella was so ugly. She had the royal artist paint several pictures of the new baby but wisely kept them under lock and key. The royal doctor tried to console the queen by saying that her daughter might grow out of it in time, but it turned out to be not so. During Dru-Ella's childhood, Bunsie taught her to crochet. This was most helpful during her dating years when she didn't.

Though Dru-Ella could not be said to be lovely, everyone knew she was kind. She was a very giving princess as well. When her potential suitors came to call, and each said "Yee-Gad!" she would always ask them if they would like tea and crumpets. And, before they left, she would give them a crocheted doily for their mothers.

It was during these disappointing years that Dru-Ella began to love the homeless and the blind. She would often stand for hours passing out cookies to hungry children in the streets. She also liked reading to the blind, who never said "Yee-Gad!" when she walked into a room.

Gradually, her kindness became known throughout the kingdom and her beauty—or lack of it—became a less noticed thing. Many began to call her The Good Princess.

All this affirmation about the good princess made Bonnie

edgy. People had quit calling her The Good Fairy and were generally just calling her The Fairy. Then one day when Bonnie was trying to change a pumpkin into a coach, it only turned into a rutabaga. It took no Mensa member to see what was abundantly clear: Bonnie was losing her powers as well as her reputation.

One day as Bonnie was walking along the street she saw some children eating cookies. "Where did you children get those cookies?" she asked.

"From the good Dru-Ella," replied the children, "and just look at the nice doilies she crocheted. What's *your* name, lady?" the children asked Bonnie. It always infuriated the defunct fairy when people didn't recognize her. So she had begun to give out her card, which read, "The *GOOD* Fairy, Bonnie." That way, they wouldn't forget her name the next time.

"Do you crochet?" the children asked.

That did it! "No, but I turn ignorant children who can't name the local good fairy into frogs!" she bellowed.

Bonnie was furious, and she cast an evil spell on the house of Sturdley. The Good Dru-Ella fell asleep under the enchantment. Bonnie made it very clear that Ms. Ugly would remain asleep until the desert froze solid or some undiscriminating prince kissed her awake, which seemed highly unlikely to happen.

Meanwhile, on the other side of a huge mountain range far from Sturdley Castle, there lived a prince named Gargoyle. He was so bony faced he had never been called "Prince Charming." Whenever he asked any maiden at the palace ball if she would like to dance, she would always say, "I'm sorry, I have arthritis."

Deep in his heart Gargoyle knew the truth. He was ugly! He brooded over his ugliness and secretly hated all the people who made him feel ugly. He inwardly despised the young girls who refused to dance with him and the children who called him "Gargoyle" instead of "Prince Gargoyle." Because people mocked him in the streets, he gradually became a hermit and let his hair and beard grow long and unkempt, making him even more repulsive than he otherwise would have been. He was lonely, nasty, and ugly. Even the people who were lonely, nasty, and ugly thought so. Still, all of his life he dreamed of meeting someone who would love him just for what he was—lonely, nasty, and ugly.

One day when he was feeling particularly ugly, he mounted his steed and rode off in search of adventure. He wandered for seven months, far across the mountains from his home. By oddest chance he happened to come upon a group of children who were wearing doilies for sun-caps. When they saw the prince they said, "Yee-Gad!" which had now become the kingdom's common greeting. The homely prince was undaunted. He asked the children where they had gotten the lovely doilies they were wearing.

"From Sleeping Ugly," they explained. They told the prince that the princess was under a spell, and that while she was quite ugly, Gargoyle might want to consider kissing her awake. "There have been no cookies in the streets since the Good Dru-Ella fell under Bonnie's evil spell. Furthermore, there are no doilies either," said one of the children.

"Prince Gargoyle," said another of the children, "this will be no storybook romance. Dru-Ella Sturdley is not what you'd call beautiful. But on the other hand, Gargoyle, you're not exactly what people would call 'Prince Charm—' "
The child choked his near blunder into silence.

The prince asked the way to the castle. When he arrived

at the castle, Olaf showed him personally to the chamber of the comatose Dru-Ella. The prince asked him to leave the two of them alone. King Olaf withdrew, leaving Prince Gargoyle and Sleeping Ugly together. Gargoyle studied her face for a long time. He had never kissed a girl, even a comatose girl, before. He started to pucker and realized that puckering made him look even uglier, for when he puckered, the bristly wart on his upper lip grew as purple as the veins on his bony face.

"Oh, never mind," he said as he unpuckered. Then he spoke to Sleeping Ugly. "My dearest Dru-Ella. They say that you are ugly, but I cannot believe it. I have seen children eating who once were hungry, and I know you gave them to eat. I have seen your lovely doilies, spun like golden spider fiber, glistening in the sun. It is not possible that one who reads to the blind and feeds the hungry could ever be ugly except to people who are so beautiful, they're vain."

He paused and studied her for a long time. "No, Dru-Ella, you are beautiful. I hesitate to kiss you, for I am truly ugly, made so by selfishness and petty hatred.

"I shall draw my blade, and then I shall kiss you. If you wake and cry, 'Yee-Gad!' then I shall slay myself. But if there is room in your good heart for one like me, then by God's good grace I will love you for all eternity." Prince Gargoyle repuckered and kissed her on the lips.

The same instant he kissed Dru-Ella, Bonnie—long cobwebbed-over in the dungeon of Sturdley Castle—felt a sharp pain in her neck. She knew her evil spell had been broken.

Sleeping Ugly awoke, and seeing Prince Gargoyle still puckered, she said, "Again, please!" This time Prince Gargoyle really kissed her in a lingering, lippy lock-up. Their

70

arms wound around each other in a desperate and clutching embrace. It was the longest kiss ever performed by those who rarely did it.

When the long, long kiss finally ended, Dru-Ella looked deep into his eyes and said, "Gargoyle, my dear sweet prince, you've come. Bonnie thought she had cast a spell over the house of Sturdley. How wrong she has been. Her spell was really worthless; I have only been *pretending* to be in a coma. I was waiting for you, Gargoyle. I never knew your name, but I knew someday you'd come, for I felt that deep within my heart, God had made someone just like you just for someone just like me. I knew we would find each other, and the pain of human rejection that we had both known would teach the world what true beauty is.

"My dearest, there is so much hurt in our kingdoms. I have discovered that when people are in real pain, they do not even care about such words as *pretty* and *ugly*. For true beauty is not made by strutting in front of mirrors. I have only two questions for you, Gargoyle. First, can you lay by your royal robes and come with me to help the poor and tend to the sick and read to the blind?"

"My lovely Dru-Ella, you know I can!"

"Don't overdo the adjectives, Gargoyle. Just call me *dear* Dru-Ella! *Lovely* is neither true nor necessary. My second question is a bit forward, but will you marry me? There will be no photographers at the wedding. I couldn't stand having an album of pictures that no one ever asked to see."

"My dear Dru-Ella, here is my crown," said Gargoyle as he took it off and threw it down. The clattering crown dropped out of sight and rolled through a huge grating in the floor. As it disappeared, the prince shouted, "I am free of you, you worthless old crown: you were always cold in the winter and heavy all year long."

They were married.

Bonnie didn't go to the wedding.

Just as Dru-Ella expected, no one said, "What a fine-looking couple you make."

Just as Gargoyle expected, nobody said, "What a lovely bride you have." But something new was loose in the kingdom. It was a spirit—a sense of true beauty.

Gargoyle and Dru-Ella honeymooned for two weeks in a leper colony, reading self-esteem books to lepers in the streets. After their honeymoon the royal couple came back home to Sturdley Castle to see what needed to be done there.

There was an outbreak of plague during their first year of marriage. Most of the sick took hope from seeing Gargoyle and Dru-Ella walking in the streets. The royal couple never wore rich robes, but there was something kingly and queenly about them. Their realm was happy, for their subjects knew that their king and queen loved them and would both live and die for them.

Cosmetic sales across the next few years dropped to zero, for the people of the realm had found a way of life that was most beautiful, a way of life that didn't depend on what one brushed on one's face or stuck in one's hair.

In time, Dru-Ella and Gargoyle had children. As one would expect, heredity won out. Their children looked a lot like them, but the people of the village called them "the children of Dru-Ella and Gargoyle" because the words *ugly* and *pretty* were no longer in common usage. Even to this day they are not to be found in the dictionaries of that wonderful and happy land.

Little Boy, Where Are You?

*In the spirit of a James Kavanaugh poem, I wrote this poem. It was my privilege to lead the Green Bay Packers in team worship on Thanksgiving Day, 1994, just before their game with Dallas. As a part of that worship service, I read this piece, written for the occasion. I remain convinced that public opinion often spoils the innocence most of us need to be winners.
—November 20, 1994*

Little boy, where are you?

I've been looking everywhere for you.
I got a big game today,
and I want to play football
like you used to play it.
I need you back!
What I really liked about you, little boy,
was that you got excited about the right things,
like flexing that little lump of a bicep
and asking your dad to feel it.
I liked the way
you sawed back and forth over the center bar
of your bike,
wobbling your way to the market with your
pant leg rolled up
so you wouldn't get your jeans caught in the chain.
I liked the way you cried about the right things:
you cried when your puppy got run over,

not when you read the sports page
after a dumb play on Saturday.
Back then you didn't limit your french fries, either,
'cause grease and salt tasted good together.
And you didn't worry about what people you didn't like
said about you
because it was real stupid to try to please the people
you didn't like.
You kept your goals simple, too,
because you knew that the things you needed
to make you really happy
were pretty simple,
like finding that first black hair
that told you you'd someday be like your daddy,
or
when the corner grocer gave you a king-sized Baby Ruth
because you played so well,
or
when your junior high coach
welcomed you into manhood by using
that not-too-bad cuss word that said, we men
gotta use them kind of words
so we won't sound too much like girls.
I need you back, little boy,
I've been looking everywhere for you
because I can still remember
that thin little arm in an oversized sleeve
that threw that ball so you could win.
You threw good back then.
Your pass wobbled a little bit,
and you couldn't get it as far down field
as you wanted it to go.
Still, it was a good pass.

And you felt good when you threw it.
And good was how you dreamed, too.
Back then you played football because you loved it,
not because you had signed a contract to do it.
You played good
because your mind was as clean as your heart,
and nobody had junked it up
by selling you some bogus national image
of your best television angles or instant replays.
I need you back, little boy.
I've gotten too concerned about how I look
and whether or not I'll get off the bench
and how I'll explain myself to the board
and whether or not I'll get invited to the press
conference.
I've forgotten how to do my own driving.
I've forgotten how to be my own man.
Where are you, little boy?
It's Thanksgiving;
I've got to play a big game;
I've been looking everywhere for you.

THE DISCIPLINE OF A SERVANT

One Sunday, after I had preached a sermon on self-sacrifice, I noticed how everyone immediately hurried off to the malls and cafeterias to indulge themselves with food and shopping sprees. Most Western Christians are trapped between Christ's call to sacrifice and their own indulgent lifestyles.—August 5, 1986

I'm but a cash-card saint in celluloid.
Can I afford to call this Jesus, King?
I'd like to follow him and yet avoid
Cross lugging and a naked death. I sing
Therefore to harmonize and think of all
I'll eat when singing's over with. Born twice,
By hundreds, then, we gather at the mall
And bless the church, or clap, or criticize.

Grace by installment—total faith—and we
Can spot a bargain when there's one in town—
The maximum of everything that's free—
With nothing but the minimum paid down.

It makes his love so interest-free! Not hard!
Like taking up your cross by Mastercard.

The Diet

It's hard for me not to try to get God and the devil
involved in my binge-and-diet lifestyle. Heaven must be
the place for glorified bodies, and hell the last resort of
those who find themselves powerless before a pan of
brownies.

I'm thirty-five sit-ups behind for the week;
I'm killing myself by degrees
By trying to jog for a mile and a half
On Rye Crisp and dry cottage cheese.

The chocolates I ate on Valentine's Day
And the homemade ice cream in July
And the turkey and eggnog I should have dismissed,
Have joined with the ugly mince pie.

And now I atone in sweatshirt and pants
(My attitude, squarely, is blah);
I pedal my old cycle-ciser a mile
With the tension set "Ooh lah, lah."

Of leg drops, I've done a full twenty-five
(On twenty I wanted to die),
And then when it's time for my celery-stick break,
I drink diet cola and cry.

If we could but look for a moment or two
On all that heaven must be,

We'd find it eternally brownies and cream—
Delicious, but calorie free.

And hell would be horror—a vast, ghastly land—
With well-worn, old bathroom scales,
Where chubbies weighed every five minutes
And jogged and ate lettuce and wailed.

THE MUFFIN MAN

In a world of sexual indulgence, self-control is an act of love, offered on the altar of self-denial.

Murray was fourteen before he really began to notice muffins. He was seventeen when they became a roaring issue in his life. His compulsion for muffins came upon him all at once in late adolescence. His whole world, it seemed to him, had begun to center around them. It wasn't just bakeries that tempted him. Everyone sold muffins: cafés and restaurants, bars and service stations, 7-Elevens and bus depots.

It was Madison Avenue that really seemed to go berserk. Muffins were used to sell everything from cologne to carburetors. Murray saw huge billboards that said, "Fly Acapulco," and sure enough, right there on the billboard would be a picture of a muffin. The muffins always looked good! Many books had muffins pictured on the dust-jacket photos. And you didn't have to read any novel very far before the hero and heroine sat down to huge helpings of muffins. The more muffins that found their way into novels, the better the books sold. Those that were best-sellers had muffins on every page, often in fits of desperate mouth-cramming, choking noises.

The theaters even rated their films. Certain letters meant "Approved for Children—No Muffins." Others meant "No Kids Allowed—Muffins in Every Scene." Most never used the word *muffins* in the title, but you knew that muffins sold tickets. Some movies—being quite up-front about the content—called a muffin a muffin. They were called "Muffins, Lies & Videotape" or "Everything You Always Wanted to Know about Muffins But Were Afraid to Ask" or "Life with the Opposite Muffin."

Murray would have gone on living in a muffin-saturated world except that he went to church. There the preacher would say, "Keep away from all this godless muffinizing. Yes, brothers and sisters: bran, blueberry, rye, raisin, or raw cocoa—all are depraved." He'd often end his sermon with the story of a beautiful young girl who laid down her Bible and fell into a life of dissipated muffinizing that led her into the gutters of gluttony.

On Sundays Murray listened to the sermons and agreed to avoid the epidemic of muffin mania that was sweeping the country. But on Mondays it was harder to carry out his resolution. He was, after all, a youth, and muffins were the singular preoccupation of the young.

What was he to do?

One Friday he went to the gym and shot a few baskets. While dressing, he heard the guys talking about the weekend muffins they were going to enjoy. He knew they'd all meet again on Monday and the muffin report would come in. Murray had a date set up for that evening, but he was determined to keep it muffin free. His date's name was Helen. She was a beautiful young woman he had met at church. In merely thinking of her, muffin mania settled over Murray.

On the night of the date, he took her to a movie. There were plenty of muffins in it. He took her out for dessert and then home. Beads of perspiration broke out all over him. "Helen," he said as they drove up to her house, "about muffins . . ." Murray's resolve began to slip. He looked at Helen hopefully, but she was resolute.

"Murray," she said, "those who eat dessert first, spoil the banquet of life. Never think of muffins before dinner. Never say 'I want' before you say 'I do.' Muffins are incredibly good, but never out of season."

They kissed good night. They dated again and again. Murray usually thought about muffins the entire time he was with Helen, but he rarely said so.

After a courtship of two years, Murray took Helen to the altar. He kissed her after they played Trumpet Voluntary and "O Promise Me." They cut the cake and drank punch. They opened gifts and flew away to Niagara Falls. They never spoke of muffins in public, but if ever a couple could be said to know the contentment and fullness of muffins, it was Murray and Helen. To everything there is a season, of course, and those who wait to bless their muffins are far too wise to speak of them in the shallow company of gluttons who devour the dough because the oven takes too long.

POOR LITTLE JACK

*One psychologist, whose lore I honor, says that men
think about sex 75 percent of our waking time. Given
this universal masculine affliction, parents ought to be
somewhat tolerant. Little Jack Horner was no doubt
cornered by a lot of appetites. He makes me wish some
parents could be more understanding.*

Little Jack Horner sat in the corner,
Clouded and thoroughly vexed.
Full well he knew, he had broken taboo
By asking his mother of sex.

"Jack," she screamed. "Lad, you are filthy and bad
To ask such a question as that!
The thoughts you employ are X-rated, boy.
Your father will give you a spat."

So Jack had to find he had a foul mind
For asking his question on sex,
And so there began to develop a man
With a devious kind of complex.

Confused now and then, Jack never again
Could question his mother gone mad.
Her reprimand stern had helped him to learn
That sex was all ugly and bad.

Confident, sure, he grew more mature,
But the sex-ban had its affect.
It became very true Jack always withdrew
From all future mention of sex.

Years had gone by, when in dickey and tie,
Jack stood at the altar with pride.
The reception was nice, and pelted with rice,
He eagerly kissed his new bride.

Something went wrong—it didn't last long—
Though no one ever knew why.
And no one suspects the awful complex
That caused a young marriage to die.

But the issues are steep, and the roots go quite deep
To the time when Jack was a lad.
When nobody other than his very mother
Had made him feel sex was all bad.

To the Spinning God of Jeremiah

*Once when the prophet Jeremiah went down to the
potter's house, he took me with him. In that wonderful
moment of studying the artist, I longed to become
obedient clay.*

I rise to the beckoning thumb
    of the Father of life,
And like a thin garment of gray,
    I surge past firm fingers
    and rise from the dead,
    turning clay.
I cannot tell what I shall
    be when the hand of the
    Lover quits pressing my life,
And the dizzying vertigo spins to
    a stop,
And the fiery kiln of his burning
    love
Dries me in the fixed shape of
    his desire.

I once was clay only—but no more.
After the spinning of life,
    I have become the very
    cup he chose to use
    to bring a refreshing
    to the lips of Christ:

An *Agnus Dei* thrice exalted,
A trinity of joys.

Again he lifts and yet again
And fills me evermore,
Till in *his* shining nearness
Amnesia won't recall the spin
    or the fury of that forming wheel
    that made me his forever.

To think I once was worthless clay,
Yet now a vessel that he uses
To nourish his poor world.

THE FORM OF A SERVANT

*I wonder if any of us have really seen Jesus who
haven't seen him reaching to us hands first.—August 3,
1986*

Hands. Broken, leathery, big and tough,
And weathered, hammer-gripping, sweating fists,
Quite used to driving nails into the rough
And bronze, blue-bruised where once the iron missed.
A hand's a thing of beauty, in the eye
Of those who, vision-trained, can pierce the skin
To see the steel of sturdy bones laid white,
And fragile tendons, filament and thin.

The riddle of the nails I understand—
How leathered calluses breed tougher skin,
Hiding tiny porcelain machines within
The flesh of your strong, injured, suff'ring hands.

   Your hammer-wielding fists at last grew frail
   And beckoned to each palm a killing nail.

PENTECOST REVISITED

Pentecost 1966 found me in the Brussels Cathedral of St. Michael. The holiday Mass offered me an hour of reflection as the high-church worship flew at me in two languages: Latin (which I understood only intermittently) and Flemish (which I understood not at all). Thirty of us tourists had gathered in the front of this great cathedral, which stretched cavernous and dark behind us.

The Eucharist was most medieval and colorful. The office was read by a red-robed cardinal attended by two Swiss guards. With all its officious gallantry and the plumage of the worship leader, the great church seemed to embarrass the little crowd huddled at the altar end of the cathedral. The ghostly echoes of the holy words flew through the vacuous and dank air of the middle-earth stones.

In my thoughts I fashioned the unintelligible service to be about the Holy Spirit, so I thumbed my English Bible to the second chapter of Acts and tried to keep faith with the cardinal, who was totally unaware that a Baptist from America was there, spying on his litany and very much in need of a word from the Lord.

No matter! It was Pentecost: a day for celebrating that time when power once fell upon the church. The wind blew then, the flame danced, too. Indeed, the miter of the bishop was in the shape of flame to recall the descent of the warm, indwelling God. On this day, in this place, the infilling and overarching presence of the Trinity came slashing across the language barriers to reveal himself to me.

The bishop swung the censer, and the odor of incense drifted from the altar, heady as a drink of new wine. I suddenly understood why the early churches were accused of a giddy and immoderate inebriation. Those whom the Spirit washed were drunk on God. They were elated, out of touch with their business-for-business, commerce-controlled world. They danced the streets mad with joy, speaking in languages they'd never learned to foreigners from countries they'd never visited. Thus Pentecost was born in this *mysterium tremendum*.

The scene from the second chapter of Acts swam in my reverie, calling to mind a rustic Oklahoma tent revival, where I first met the Holy Spirit two decades earlier. I was nine years old in the year when World War II ended. *Hiroshima* and *Nagasaki* each sounded a little like Native American tribes, and each had the same number of syllables as *Oklahoma*. I couldn't imagine exactly where they were, but the whole world had come to focus on their desperation. The adults in my world talked of little else. Pictures of these places, under headline letters thick as my young fingers, covered the newspapers black with smudgeable ink. My four older brothers-in-law would soon come home, those headlines said. Indeed, we thanked God that the possibility of their dying had passed.

In that very year of joy and cataclysm, the Pentecostals erected a tent. (There was little use in asking where the Pentecostals got their tents. It was like asking where Ringling Brothers got *their* tents. Pentecostals had tents, that was all!) And they came to *our* town. Their big-top tabernacle rose above a swampy, snaky tent site and was as wind billowed as the happy accordion sounds that filled the canvas like sails. The tent swayed but never fell, for it was held up by staked ropes, taut as the guitar strings that played along with the reedy accordions. The tent looked like a huge orange jack-o'-lantern, lit by dangling light-bulbs, around which swarmed the candle-flies of August. Always with August came revivals, as medicine shows came with June. Both "shows" peddled their wares in canvas cathedrals, floored with wood chips, domed with tarpaulins, pewed with two-by-twelve boards resting on concrete blocks.

In this tent, on one of those pew boards, I found myself seated, shirtless and shoeless (you could get by with that in 1945 if you were a child. "No shoes, no shirt, no service" was sloganized by restaurants, not Pentecostals). Worst of all, I was not "saved." Oklahoma Pentecostals had divided all the world into two broad categories: saved and unsaved. By the age of nine I, and most everyone else, knew which category was mine. Indeed, that's why we had tent revivals, so people could change categories.

The person who helped change the categories was the Holy Spirit. That was what the Spirit did: he helped the lost get saved, and the saved act more like it. Most of the *dramatis personae* of this rural drama now escape me. I do remember two huge Gepettos who played monstrous John Deere-sized accordions. There was also an unforgettable reformed drunkard who, through streaming tears, told how he had been set free of the devil's power. One of the athletic evangelists wore a leather buckskin coat, whose swishing, dangling strips of cowhide fringe lured the eye hypnotically as he made the earth tremble with his gargantuan glossolalia.

I listened, sincerely and with fear. Who wouldn't? As Nagasaki yet smoldered, this red-eyed prophet told us of the great whore of Babylon who would fornicate with the

Antichrist till blood flowed to the horses' bridles. I trembled as he warned us to make ready for apocalyptic hordes of frogs and locusts. After that, the Euphrates River would go bone-dry like the Salt Fork (a sun-dried riverbed of northern Oklahoma), he said. Then Gog and Magog would rise up, and the real tribulation would begin to tribulate. I quailed wide-eyed as the buckskin jacket rippled on the chest of this doomsdayer who spoke with authority (which was something, he implied, the liberal denominations did *not* do).

This matter was serious. The hymns made me as nervous as the preaching, for they were rapturously exultant about death and all the great things that would come once we had all had the good fortune to die. "Some glad morning when this life is o'er, I'll fly away," said one hymn. Another rhapsodized, "Almost cannot avail, almost is but to fail, sad, sad the bitter wail, almost but lost." But the song that choked my voice to silence went, "I was sinking deep in sin, far from the peaceful shore, very deeply stained within, sinking to rise no more." Oh, the pain I felt as the hymns and the accordions lamented my childhood fate. I saw only "the dark wave"; Oh, how I needed "the lifeline to be saved."

"In nomine Patris, et Filii, et Spiritus Sancti"; the cardinal changed the thread that bound the Mass in Brussels to my aimless mental travels back into my childhood years. While his Latin office rolled by, I wondered if the cardinal knew some of those old tent hymns like "Farther Along" and "I'll Fly Away." His red robe fascinated me and so did the medieval garb of the beefeaters, who stood like altar guards, staring into the long, dark cavern of St. Michael's. The cardinal's robe swished as he pivoted and Latinated. Suddenly I realized how different his dress was from the

90

buckskins of the evangelist who preached in the Pentecostal tent. *We all have our own denominational costumes,* I thought. Suddenly he lifted the cup, genuflected, and spoke again of the *Spiritus Sanctus.* Somehow I knew we were brothers: he had convinced me he was "saved."

I'm not sure he would have convinced the evangelist or Sister Rose, our Pentecostal pastor. She, too, was at the revival that Shechinah night when Nagasaki burned in the news and another fierce fire burned in my heart. She, too, knew the Spirit; I could tell. Sister Rose didn't play around at being religious. She clamped her eyes shut and lifted her head as though she could see through both her clenched eyelids and the canvas that domed our primitive glory. *"Shandala,"* she glossolised. Tears streamed down her face. Sister Rose was truly "filled" with the Holy Ghost. Even Sister Rodgers said so, and Sister Rodgers had the gift of discernment, which meant that she, more than others, could tell who truly was filled and who wasn't.

I wasn't. Sister Rodgers would know that too, of course. So when they began to sing "O Why Not Tonight?" it seemed an honest question unblemished by the adenoidal alto harmony that always marked our singing of the invitation. "Step forward to the altar, so you'll never have to step into hell," shouted the buckskinned evangelist above the plaintive singing. Sister Rose was weeping. Sister Rodgers was discerning. The burden was immense. I broke into tears. Emotion burned like fire through the sawdust chips.

Hell, dark as a gospel tent in a power outage, suddenly gaped like a black hole before me. I stood weeping, naked, foolish, and undone. What would I do if God should bring Gog to Garfield County? I knew not when Christ would come! Lucky for me, they sang an invitation: "O do not let the Word depart, and close thine eyes against the light, poor sinner harden not your heart, be saved, oh, tonight."

I had no choice. I had to fly to the arms of Jesus. I did. Wonder of wonders, he did all the hymn said: he snatched my feet from the fiery clay and set me on the rock. I changed categories. I was saved.

That wood-chip aisle was a kind of yellow brick road that ended in Oz. I was saved, said Sister Rose, but Sister Rodgers said I was filled. They were both right, of course, said Brother Buckskin, and I felt a marvelous elation. What happened to me then in Garfield County was described by the reading of the book of Acts in the Brussels cathedral:

> And when the day of Pentecost was fully come, they were all with one accord in one place. And suddenly there came a sound from heaven as of a rushing mighty wind, and it filled all the house where they were sitting. And there appeared unto them cloven tongues like as of fire, and it sat upon each of them. And they were all filled with the Holy Ghost, and began to speak with other tongues, as the Spirit gave them utterance . . . Others mocking said, These men are full of new wine. . . .
>
> But Peter, standing up with the eleven, lifted up his voice, and said unto them, Ye men of Judaea, and all ye that dwell at Jerusalem, be this known unto you, and harken to my words: For these are not drunken, as ye suppose, seeing it is but the third hour of the day. But this is that which was spoken by the prophet Joel; And it shall come to

pass in the last days, saith God, I will pour out of my Spirit upon all flesh: and your sons and your daughters shall prophesy, and your young men shall see visions, and your old men shall dream dreams: And on my servants and on my handmaidens I will pour out in those days of my Spirit; and they shall prophesy: And I will shew wonders in heaven above, and signs in the earth beneath; blood, and fire, and vapour of smoke: The sun shall be turned into darkness, and the moon into blood, before that great and notable day of the Lord come: And it shall come to pass, that whosoever shall call on the name of the Lord shall be saved. (KJV)

The cardinal did not seem nearly as moving as Sister Rose had seemed. Still, I felt the years condense: 1945 and 1966 were one. That's what the Spirit does: he condenses, integrates, and unifies all years and all saving experience. We see this with the prophet Joel's words that bind the ages before Christ with Peter's ecstatic sermon of A.D. 27 and with Chrysostom, Augustine, Aquinas, and yes, Sister Rose. To be sure, all ages, cultures, and churches go about it differently, but we are yet made one by the *Spiritus Sanctus*.

Suddenly I understood: Pentecost is not merely a day on the church calendar; it is fire and wind able to blow and burn anytime. The elation is inebriating. It comes suddenly like the wind of which Jesus said, "The wind bloweth where it listeth, and thou hearest the sound thereof, but canst not tell whence it cometh, and whither it goeth: so is every one that is born of the Spirit" (KJV). And, like the Jerusalem pilgrims in the book of Acts, our elation must make us appear as though we have gotten "drunk on God," and the joy binds the ages. Jesus, in the Gospel of John passage on the Spirit, speaks of being born again. The Acts passage on the Spirit ends with a mass conversion of pilgrims. Conversion is always the first, best work of the Spirit of God.

In my life it was true. I wondered about the priest. How did he come to know the Spirit? How diverse must be the ways of God to make an educated cardinal and a bashful child of nine one in Christ. Still, this is his most glorious work, unitive across our wide differences.

I have an older friend who helped liberate Belsen, the German concentration camp, in 1945. He said that as he leaned against a wall of execution, he looked out at the newly silent concentration camp and saw the grim reminder of man's inhumanity. The greatness of the moment overcame him, and the Spirit soared into his life. C. S. Lewis came more gradually to know the Spirit's reality. He wrangled on a bus top and in a motorcycle sidecar with the very God whose existence his mind tried to deny! But, no matter the circumstance, the Spirit's coming is authentic in however and whenever it occurs.

But what of the cardinal? What of me? The coming of the Spirit in my life certainly lacks the historical grandeur of a conversion at the liberation of Belsen. As a child, I merely knelt between two big Pentecostal women in the sawdust, and there he came. But the experience is as indelible as what Acts describes as "young men having visions, and old men dreaming dreams, and women preaching the glory of his coming."

While I thought about these things, the cardinal all too abruptly swished away; the Mass was over. In a way I felt cheated. The wafer and wine were not for me, a Protestant. Church doctrine can sometimes mar a beautiful experience, but while it might bar me from the table, an experience of faith had been opened. I walked out of the dark church. The sun drenched the world with glorious sunlight, which, like the Spirit, unified the world with brightness. The costumes were gone; the congregation was back in the streets. Neon blinked its glitzy enticement from bistro to bistro.

Never mind!

There was a fire loose in the world that made Jerusalem, Oklahoma, and Belgium all one. It wasn't as obvious as I might have liked outside the cathedral. But the integrating Spirit was there . . . and would always be. Who knows where the wind may yet blow? Where the flame may yet surprise us? Such a fire is ever in us even when it hides, waiting to reveal itself where the coldness of reason freezes.

SONG OF THE ROBE-TOUCHER
GOSPEL OF LUKE 8:43-48

December 27, 1970

I struggled just to touch
Him, in my frail attack
Against the crowd so much around.
They shoved me back.

In weakened fury there
I tore the people wall.
I clawed the frenzied air.
The Savior seemed so tall.

Yet through that madding crowd,
I could not seem to probe
The human press. I'd vowed
My hand should touch his robe.

And then the instant came!
The wall gave way. The tide
Fell back. I breathed his name
In freedom at his side.

I fell with hands outstretched
And felt his tunic there.
The crowd moved by a wretch
Who breathed a strange new air.

FRIDAY AND SUNDAY

Hurry Easter!

Friday

Pull out the nails from His gripless hands;
Loosen the ropes from the shoulders of this man;
Take Him from the wood and lay Him on the sand.
He is dead—it is Friday—He is dead!

The woman who is weeping said He was her son;
Said He was forepromised as the Mighty One;
Thirty years of motherhood, all undone.
Weep, little mother—He is dead.

Prostitutes and publicans, weep and rave;
Your King who gave you life is ready for the grave;
Lay your cold Messiah in a cold, dark cave.
Weep, you hapless orphans—He is dead.

"Dead," moaned the chilling April wind;
"Dead," sobbed the Pharisee who was His friend;
Dead—immortality has met its end.
Eternal life is done with—He is dead.

All of you fishers, return to the sea;
You were His disciples until Calvary;
Weep your weary way back to Galilee.
He has cried, "It is finished," and is dead.

The promises of victory have ended in defeat;
Friday's Conqueror has pierced feet;
He is bound in a shroud and a winding sheet.
The Carpenter of Nazareth is dead.

Sunday

Look! Shafts of sunlight have driven back the night.
Look at the Master clothed in iridescent white.
Look at the women falling back in fright.
He's alive—It is Sunday—He's alive!

Rejoice, James and John and Simon of Cyrene,
Peter, Nicodemus, and Mary Magdalene:
Annas and Cleopas the risen Lord have seen.
He is living—He is living—He's alive!

Oh, Thomas, Thomas, why do you doubt?
Thrust in your hand where the spear came out;
This is not a fantasy. Lift the joyous shout.
He is living—He is living—He's alive!

Flourish the trumpets; the living Savior comes.
Roll the victory cadence on a thousand drums.
Let the anthem swell from a thousand tongues.
He is living—He is living—He's alive!

IV. DEFECTIVE COMPONENTS

IV. Defective Components

Faith Imperfections

Scrambled Humanity

Defective Components

"ALL THAT GOD DOES IS DONE WELL," said Rabbi Akiba. Was the sage right? If so, how do we explain the ghastly imperfections of our inhumane sociology? There is always the problem of evil. Theologians call the struggle *theodicy*. Theodicy deals with ugly discrepancies such as "Why do bad things happen to good people?" or questions as trivial as "If there really is a God, why am I stuck in the 5:30 traffic?" But the questions can be gut wrenching, as in the case of the mother who asks, "Why was my child born with this defect?" The grand indictment of these questions falls against God. But I am more offended by those blasé scholars who ask the question, "What happened to God's goodness?" It is the cynic more than the paraplegic who calls my attention to the issue of damaged components.

God, in his perfection, formed us. Sometime after our creation, many of us become snobs or pharisees, traitors or cynics. But we were made better than we have become. Somewhere along the line we have to find that when our philosophy is squarely bolted to the structure of our worldview, the framework of our faith needs to be modified to fit its foundation. Sometimes old concepts that once appeared strong have to be wrenched from our naïveté because they are too weak to support all we require of them.

What is to be done with defective components? Much wrangling over the nature of God's character can destroy the smooth operation of our lives. Therefore, before adopting any idea, check each new component of your worldview for flaws and fissures that could cost you years of forward progress.

Life never becomes defective when it is focused on God's values. We see this as foundational in the book of Philippians, where we are told, "Finally, brothers, whatever is true, whatever is noble . . . , whatever is lovely, whatever is admirable—if anything is excellent or praiseworthy— think about such things."

Jesus was pretty specific about ordering us not to judge what appears to be some defective component in others. He reminded us that the severity of our own judgments would be met again in the final judgment. He took time to point out that the scribes and pharisees were getting a lot of satisfaction by looking at others' defective components. The result was a frailty of their servanthood, producing such things as self-righteousness and critical spirits.

The world is fascinated by those who transcend their defective components. Such large souls have no need to be perfect, only to serve. The following lessons were learning points in my pilgrimage. These stories bear healing, because in so many cases they enticed the raconteur to allow his narratives to heal himself. Blessed are all those still searching for a cure. Once stories have been used to heal, they are ready to serve as a prescription.

102

IF YOU WOULD JUST . . .

We live in misery when we cannot master the art of that
unconditional acceptance that God ever extends to us.
"Just as I am, I come" is a great hymn to sing to God.
"Just as you are, you're all right with me" is a great
hymn to sing to others.

Ethel had always had a long, long nose. In grade school
the kids all called her "Beaky" until she ran into the
restroom and cried. She was nearly thirty before Elmer
(who had a fairly long nose himself) asked her to marry
him. She said, "Yes, of course, I'll marry you, but what
about my nose?"

"What nose?" asked Elmer.

This was clearly the man for her.

She married Elmer, who loved her and never seemed to
notice the length of her nose. But Ethel was not so gracious.
Though her own nose had been fully accepted by Elmer,
she had, over the years, begun to feel that Elmer's nose
was just too long, and she didn't mind saying so.

"It's too long, Elmer!" said Ethel, looking straight at Elmer's nose. "If you would just have it clipped, you'd be a
good-looking man."

Elmer felt bad, but he trusted Ethel. Every time she said,
"Elmer, if you would just . . . ," she would tell him something that was good for him. Now she was telling him the
plain truth. His nose was too long. He could see that.

While he was thinking about the nose-clip surgery, Elmer
remembered their exchange of marriage vows. Ethel had

told him, "Elmer, if you would just say 'I do,' we both would find a real life together filled with happiness forever." And so Elmer had said, "I do."

Ethel was half right. Elmer was happy, but Ethel was ill at ease with Elmer—there were so many things wrong with him. One of the first things Ethel said to him on their honeymoon was that he snored so loud she couldn't sleep. "If you would just have your adenoids out, I could be truly happy with you." So Elmer went to an E.N.T. surgeon and had his adenoids taken out. He quit snoring, but Ethel wasn't entirely happy.

When Elmer saw her looking at his neck mole, he could have said it before she did: "Elmer, if you would just have that mole taken off your neck . . ." It wasn't much of a trick. It cost $65 in outpatient charges. Presto: no more neck mole.

The same thing happened with Elmer's overlap incisors. "Elmer, if you would just—"

"Oh, Ethel, of course," said Elmer, not letting her finish. An oral surgeon finished the task and Ethel was happy for a week or so, but soon Ethel pointed out that his tonsils were always infected and probably responsible for his halitosis. "Elmer, if you would just . . ." So, of course, he did.

He was in the basement meditating on whom he should call about the nose clip when Ethel made her way down the rickety steps and found him sitting in a dark corner. As her eyes fully adjusted to the low light, she saw a crude shelf with a sign over it. The sign said ELMER, IF YOU WOULD JUST . . . , A series of bottles sat on the shelf labeled with dates and filled with clear solutions. Inside each of the bottles were things like moles and teeth and adenoids and tonsils. On the last bottle was written "Nose tip," all ready to be dated when his surgery was over.

"Ethel . . ." Elmer hesitated, "I was about to call a plastic surgeon."

"Why, Elmer, if you would just—" Ethel stopped and looked at the sign over the shelf. Suddenly she felt ashamed. She realized *If-you-would-just* was a terrible game. "Elmer, if you would just . . . ," she went on, "postpone that nose clip. I want to get mine clipped first."

"But, darling, I like your nose the way it is!"

"Elmer, are you sure?"

He stood up and kissed her sweetly on the tip of her long proboscis. "Ethel, I know how to make our marriage perfect."

"I do too, Elmer, but go ahead and say it."

"If you would just quit saying, 'If you would just. . . .' "

THE SCRIBE

These fourteen lines I wrote out of appreciation for
Jesus, who must have felt the sting of those scholars
who had traded their prayers for academic pursuits.
The best scholarship is valid when joined with devotion.

Good morning, Doctor Wright. Let there be light
From the dim past. May scholarship, aflame,
Burst into gold, dispel the naïve night,
Illuminate the letters with your name.
Your hungry-minded students wait again—
Baby sparrows all—with beaks turned up.
So you may drop the Hebrew morsels in
Like academic worms from Reason's cup.

Poor scholars swilled on academic grog!
In books alone you unrewarded seek
As Yahweh rolled in scrolls of vellum sweet,
Unfurls himself for you in private synagogue.

How nice that wisdom comes to you each dawn
The moment you throw your regalia on.

106

THE PHARISEE

I offer this judgment on pharisees who made broad their academic stripes and big their phylacteries. It is a couple of millennia too late to correct their errors, so this poem is offered as counsel for their descendants.

Do you see him there? The public square
Is just the place to photograph his face
Etched with earnest lines. He weeps. He cares.
He thunders recompense, intones his grace.
We must unfold our hands and then applaud.
And gape at academic piety.
Degrees and robes can make us look like God,
Festoon us in neon humility.

ENCORE! ENCORE! Pray earnestly, God-friend.
The quadraphonic tone of your *Amen*
Will send the curtain flying up again.
The seats are packed with rapt humanity.

Kneel closer to the lights so we may see.
Dear God, is this unticketed and free?

ISCARIOT

I'm prone to be forgiving of Judas, since I so often bring to Christ my own betrayals. But when the cross is near and sweet to me, Iscariot seems reprehensible. This is how I feel about him most Good Fridays.

Traitor's tundra, barren hate,
Ice transactions which preclude us,
One name freezes Hell itself:
Barren, arctic soul of Judas.

The gibbet where the Savior died,
Ropes and steel and willow rods,
Swabbing gallows, scarlet hate:
Heinous homicide of God.

Timeless dying, timeless tears,
Timeless grace sent to include us.
Ebbing love declares the fiend:
Judas, Judas, Judas . . . JUDAS!

God slayer! Savior killer!
Grief of time made wearisome.
Butcher-fiend of love and grace!
Monster! Traitor! Evil one!

Buying God for common coin,
Shackled brute of silver curse,

Turncoat, false and killing liar,
History and bloody purse.

Wherever treachery loathes light,
And Hell seeks to include us,
Monuments in black will rise:
Heartless granite icon, Judas!

TUESDAY'S COOKIES

*Of the heartbreaking phenomena of our time, one of the
deepest heartbreaks is the abuse of children by their
parents. There is no understanding why this should be
so, but increasingly child abuse is damaging young
psyches; that damage is sometimes not repairable over
the remainder of their lives. I was often counselor to
such cases. I wrote this metaphor of hope after a
counseling session.*

Once there was a very happy little girl who had a very
respected mother and father and many wonderful friends.
Her father was named Sunday Johnson, her mother was
named Monday Johnson, and she was named Tuesday
Johnson. They had a cat named August, a dog named
Christmas, and a goldfish named Arbor Day. They all rode
to church in a red van with "HAPPY" on their vanity li-
cense plates.

One Wednesday, Monday gave her little Tuesday a beautiful little bag of cookies and left her with her father, Sunday, while she went shopping. They were Tuesday's
favorite kind of cookies, what she called "chunklate covered grab-crackers." She was so happy she began to dance
excitedly about the room, singing as she danced:

> "Chunkalated, chunkalated,
> One—two—three!
> Grab-crackers floating in a chunklate sea!

> Roll 'em in the blackberries, dip 'em in
> your tea!
> Chunklate covered grab-crackers, all for
> me!"

It was a song she sang every time she was given her favorite cookies.

While she was singing happily, her mother, Monday, left to go shopping. No sooner was Monday out of the house, than her father, Sunday, began to act very strangely. He looked out the windows and smiled on the empty streets. Then he drew all the drapes and shut out the beautiful sunlight. He took Tuesday to a corner of the couch and sat her on his lap. Then he forcefully took the cookies away from her. Tuesday was shocked when Sunday opened her sack of chunklate covered grab-crackers and broke them all in pieces. This made Tuesday feel very ashamed, and so she cried. She always cried when she felt ashamed.

Monday was confused when she came home from her shopping trip and found Tuesday crying.

"What's the matter, dear?" she asked.

"Oh, nothing," Tuesday sobbed.

But in a little while, Monday found the bag of broken cookies and gasped. "Tuesday, what happened? Who broke your beautiful cookies?"

Since Tuesday could not bring herself to say, "Daddy!" she simply looked down and said, "I did it!"

When school started in the fall, Tuesday was ashamed to open her lunch sack in front of the other children. So she always sat alone in the lunchroom. She would just sit by herself in the corner of the lunchroom holding her crumpled cookie sack, but not opening it. Her teacher, noticing this, approached her and said, "Not hungry, Tuesday?"

The teacher took her crumpled sack and pried Tuesday's fingers away from the folded bag. "Well, no wonder you're not hungry!" said her teacher. "Your cookies are pulverized. Who did this?"

"I did," lied Tuesday. Then she took some of the crumbles and started eating them, trying to act as though she preferred pulverized cookies.

And so it began to happen regularly. Many mornings after Tuesday's mother, Monday, had gone to work, her father would rise, look out the windows, and draw the drapes. Then, when all the golden sunlight was gone and the room was very dark, Sunday Johnson would take Tuesday on his lap, and one by one he would crumble her grab-crackers even more and smile and put them back in her sack, even as tears ran down her face.

But as she got older she quit crying because she found crying didn't help, and she worked very hard at loving her father. In fact, after he would break her cookies, she would smile cautiously and say, "Daddy, I love you!" She was convinced that if she said it enough, perhaps one day he would quit drawing the drapes and shutting the sunlight out of her life. But he never stopped closing the drapes, and when anyone asked her, as she sat in the corner of the lunchroom, "Who broke your cookies, Tuesday?" she would always answer, "I did."

At church, her father was a deacon. Sunday Johnson was loved and respected as a man of God with very high values. All of the church members called him "Brother Sunday." It was early in her teen-age years that Sunday quit breaking Tuesday's cookies. Her cookies were so broken and she was so emotionally scarred from all the years of cookie-breaking, that she found it hard to want to be around people. She grew very thin, ate poorly, and seemed to not

112

want to be outside or with large groups of people. The family doctor said that she needed to eat more and that, as thin as she was, it would not hurt her to eat more sweets, including all the cookies that she wanted. But she had developed a dislike for cookies, and she especially hated chunklate covered grab-crackers.

When Tuesday was a teenager, she went to a big gospel meeting where she heard her father, Sunday, preaching to a large crowd of more than 300 young people. He was preaching a very powerful sermon called "Keeping Your Cookies in One Piece!" It was the very first of a whole series on cookies. The next night, Sunday preached a very stern message called "Saving Your Cookies for that One Special Person." His sermon made Tuesday feel so guilty that she went forward to the altar while all the people sang a song called "Just as I Am." When she got to the altar, she was greeted by her father, who asked, "Why are you coming to the altar, Tuesday?"

"Because I love you, Daddy," was all she could think to say.

He said nothing in return, and she quit going to church soon after that.

In her last year of college, Tuesday met another graduating senior whom she felt was just right for her; his name was Friday Jones. He was kind and warm and always considerate. Tuesday began to fall in love with him, and they dated more and more regularly. Only once did he talk about cookies: "Would you like . . . ?"

But Tuesday threw up her hand like an officer of the law and said, "Please, please—I'm saving my cookies for the right person at the right time."

Friday laughed. "Me too. But don't look so severe about it!"

He never asked her to violate her cookie convictions, in fact, he seemed pleased that she had such convictions. But in her heart Tuesday thought to herself, *If only he knew about my smashed cookies, he would never look at me again.*

The days of their courtship flew by, and they both graduated from college. Then in August (a month that Tuesday preferred because in the part of her childhood that was happy she had a favorite cat with that name), they were married. They had a wonderful wedding. After the reception, when all of the people had gone and they had opened many wonderful presents, they flew away to Easter Island for their honeymoon.

They went to their honeymoon cottage.

Friday Jones picked up Tuesday Jones and carried her across the threshold. Then he kicked the door shut and swung her around the room, laughing in the utter joy of their wonderful marriage.

"I love you, Tuesday Johnson!" he shouted out loud in utter pride.

"Not Tuesday Johnson, never again Tuesday Johnson—I'm Tuesday Jones now!"

They kissed again.

Then as they brightly laughed, Friday pulled out a new-looking sack.

"Know what I've got here?"

Tuesday blushed, but said nothing.

"Chunklate covered grab-crackers!"

Tuesday suddenly began crying. He looked stunned as she pulled out an old crumpled sack; it was full of old, moldy, and broken cookies. For their entire honeymoon they barely said a thing. Friday closed his sack of goodies, and Tuesday shyly insisted on putting hers where he would never have to look at her poor crumpled sack again.

For the first few months after their honeymoon Friday was so kind as not to bring up the matter of cookies. But after a while Tuesday and Friday went to see Dr. Graham Bars, a counselor they had both known for a long time. He was a friend of both their families. While he was surprised to see them, he knew almost immediately why they had come. "Broken cookies?" he asked Tuesday.

"Yes," she said, looking down.

"Your father broke them, didn't he?" asked Dr. Graham Bars.

"Yes," she said again. "How did you know?"

"I've heard his severe talks on cookies, and a person who is that adamant about cookies is usually preaching sermons to himself."

They all three sat silently for a moment.

"And are you disappointed, Friday, that Tuesday has an aversion to cookies? Do you want a divorce?" asked Dr. Bars.

"No, I don't! I certainly do not! I want Tuesday; I could never want anyone else. I will always love her. And I'll wait forever till our marriage is well, but tell me this, Dr. Bars: Can you fix her broken cookies?"

"Wait here, you two," Dr. Bars said. He got up and abruptly left the room. In a moment he came back with a huge tube that had the words *Cookie Glue* on the side. "We'll use this for a few months, and we'll never quit working on this problem till the problem is fixed. It may not take as long as you think."

So Tuesday and Friday Jones and Dr. Graham Bars worked for seven months on ways to glue broken cookies together. Just when they were beginning to despair that Tuesday's cookies would ever be mended, Tuesday had an experience that was totally unexpected. It happened right after Friday went to work one morning. Tuesday was by herself, having a cup of coffee in their little apartment, when she walked to the window and looked out into the sunny street. There was a tall man standing on the sidewalk just in front of her home. He was a baker, dressed all in white. Though he said nothing, he headed toward her window and held something out to her: a brand-new sack. She thought she knew what was in the sack, but she was afraid of all men with sacks. She became so agitated she dropped her coffee cup. Tears flooded her eyes. She reached for the draw cord and closed the drapes.

Now she was terribly unnerved. She had the feeling that while she had shut the baker out in the street, he was now in the room with her. A voice broke into the darkened room around her: "It does little good to try to glue your cookies together while your soul is unglued. The guilt you bear was never yours."

"But all my cookies are broken—*I* am broken . . . soiled . . . despised. . . ."

"Those words are for me to bear, not you. Your words are *whole, clean,* and *loved.*"

"Then give me my words, and I will be healed!"

The words were barely out of her mouth when the darkness in the room was shattered by a blinding light. For a while the blue-white incandescence forbade her eyes to adjust. However, as her sight gradually returned, she felt well: as though she were healed. *"Whole, clean,* and *loved.* These are my words!" she shouted. She whirled around the room as delirious with joy as though she were a child. In a pirouette of joy, she grabbed the draw cord of the drapes and swished the curtains wide open. Sunlight flew into the room like a tidal wave of newness.

And then she saw it: sitting on the table, awfully close to the Bible she had carried in her wedding. It was there! A sack! A crisp, new sack! And on the side it said simply, "Bon Appetit! The Baker!" Tremblingly she opened the bag. She knew it. There they were: whole and unbroken chunklate covered grab-crackers!

Tears flowed freely down her cheeks as she reached for the phone and dialed. As she waited for someone to answer, she found herself wanting to sing. At length the receptionist at Friday's office answered. "This is Tuesday Jones. May I speak to Friday?" she asked. After another wait, she was connected to him. "Friday, darling, this is Tuesday. I've something wonderful to show you! I know you have lots to do at the office, but could you get home as early as possible today?" He seemed stunned by her exuberance but agreed to get home as early as possible. "I love you, Friday Jones," she laughed.

All day long, Friday wondered what Tuesday's big surprise was going to be. He dared to hope that somehow her dreadful struggles of soul were over. She sounded so happy that he himself remained bouyant for most of the day. When he finally walked up to the door of his apartment, he noticed that Tuesday had already set the trash out for the collectors the next morning. There in the top of the container he saw the half-used tube of Cookie Glue. *Good,* he thought to himself. *That stuff wasn't working, anyway!*

He was about to open the door and walk in when he heard singing from inside. Tuesday was singing a little song he had never heard her sing before. It was an odd song, a familiar—yet somehow new—cookie rhyme:

"Chunkalated, chunkalated!
One—Two—Three . . ."

Friday smiled as he opened the door. There stood Tuesday holding out toward him a brand-new sack of cookies. He took her in his arms, cookies and all. He was delighted.

With the passing of time, all of their neighbors knew there was no happier couple in the world, and often when Friday and Tuesday were together cooking out or enjoying the last warm days of summer, they could be heard singing that old nursery rhyme of children whose lives are happy in spite of shadows:

> "Chunkalated, chunkalated,
> One—Two—Three!
> Grab-crackers floating in a chunklate sea!
> Roll 'em in blackberries, dip 'em in your tea!
> Chunkalated grab-crackers all for me!"

THE BROKEN THING

*Most of us are vessels that cannot hold the will of God
until we're shattered and re-assembled. Brokenness
comes first, usability later.*

The little broken fragments
Lay so useless on the floor—
Lots of tiny fractured pieces,
And the vessel is no more.

Silver slivers of ceramic,
And no one can comprehend
Any way to mold the pieces
That the vessel serve again.

Then comes the master craftsman
Hovering o'er the broken clay,
For he will not see it useless,
And cast carelessly away.

With skill, his able fingers
Reach to lift the pieces up,
Pick the fragments from the floor,
Fit them back into the cup.

He will use the cup made whole again,
To make his heart to sing,
For he can restore to usefulness
Such shattered, broken things.

A Certain Priest

Sin is serious business, but then so is grace.

Every day on his way to hear morning confessions, a certain priest stopped and stole an apple from an orchard that he passed. On the orchard wall was a sign that clearly said, "Keep Out, No Pilfering!" Nonetheless, the priest would steal the fruit and eat it on the way to serve his people. He always finished the apple just as he entered the confessional, throwing the apple core on *his* side of the curtain.

A young girl named Cora also stopped every morning on her way to confession to steal an apple. Entering the confessional, she would finish the apple and throw the core on *her* side of the curtain.

"Bless me, Father, for I have sinned," she would say.

"How long has it been, my child, since your last confession?"

"Twenty-four hours."

"And is your sin the same today as usual?"

"It is, Father. I am still stealing apples on the way to confession."

"Te absolvo. Go, and try to keep away from those apples!"

"I'll try, Father, I'll try. But they are so good, and I am so weak."

Every day the ritual was repeated. Every twenty-four hours the priest stole another, and so did Cora.

Finally the priest grew exasperated with Cora. "Bless me, Father, for I have sinned," she said: a very ordinary confession on an ordinary morning.

"Today, Cora, I refuse to forgive you. You keep on stealing, and I'm tired of forgiving you, for we both know you will do it again. You'll never change, you wretched girl. Henceforth, I do not forgive you."

"Please, Father. I'm so very sorry."

"No. Before the cider dries upon your chin, you will have stolen once again. I counted 365 decaying cores on your side of the confessional. You are too wicked and apple-ridden to ever receive my forgiveness!"

The girl wept her way from the confessional. For weeks her guilt grew. She finally quit coming to confession.

Autumn came. Winter approached.

The fields around the church turned brown. The swans left the pond. The early daylight was heavy with frost. The apples in the orchard were very few and mostly in the top of the trees. The wretched girl, still unable to leave her addiction, shinnied up to the highest frost-tinged boughs. She was about to pick an apple when she noticed some movements in the branches across from her. Then she noticed a black cassock.

"Father, what are you doing here?" asked Cora.

"Praying," said the priest.

"In an apple tree?" asked the girl.

"Yes, my dear, to be closer to heaven."

"Oh, that I came here to pray . . . I came only to steal apples."

"Wretch!" screamed the priest.

At that very instant the limb on which he was supported broke, and the priest plummeted to the ground. Cora scrambled down and ran to see if the priest was dead.

"Girl, I am dying. You must give me last rites."

"No, Father. I am impure, filled with harried and vile

and unforgiven apple thieveries. I am too wicked to grant you the absolution that you need. May God have mercy on you, Father."

The priest died and went to hades and burned in flaming cider for a thousand years—but of course Cora never knew.

A new priest came in a few weeks, and Cora started back to church. Once again she went to confession.

"Bless me, Father, for I have sinned. . . . I stole an apple this morning on the way to church."

"You, too?" said the priest. "Tomorrow morning let's both steal three, and we shall make a pie together. Who knows but that our Father in heaven shall provide the cinnamon."

Even honest thievery had recompenses. At last the swans came back and the fields turned green.

After Cora and the priest had eaten many a pie, they found they actually were beginning to help each other deal with their problems. They leaned on each other for support and prayed for each other, and finally both were able to quit stealing apples—at least they did not steal them all that often. Still, some sins are hard to quit, and confirmed apple thieves must help each other past the best orchards.

V. What You Can Expect from the Product

V. What You Can Expect from the Product

WHAT YOU CAN EXPECT FROM THE PRODUCT

LIFE'S NOT ALWAYS EASY TO ASSEMBLE.
Just when you think all the pieces fit, you discover the whole assembly is a bit off. A kind of dread occupies your thoughts. You have the overwhelming feeling that nothing will ever make sense again. " 'Meaningless! Meaningless!' says the Teacher. 'Utterly meaningless! Everything is meaningless.' All things are wearisome, more than one can say. The eye never has enough of seeing, nor the ear its fill of hearing.' "

What puts life back together? Grace!

Grace is the healing generosity of God that touches us so powerfully that nothing is ever quite the same again.

Grace is never-to-be-deserved, yet grace assembles the odd pieces of our lives, and we are made whole.

Grace is the love we get when we were not expecting anything. God smiles upon us for reasons we never understand, and where he smiles, grace is born. It comes down like the gentle rain from heaven when our souls are parched, and nourishes all that it touches.

There is a disconsolation that comes to us all when we face what philosophers call "the medusa of existence." What does life mean? Isn't Christianity supposed to be a religion of meaning? Do we have all the pieces to fit our purpose together? What may we reasonably expect from Christianity?

First of all, we can expect this grace to transform us. We cannot encounter the Manufacturer's grace without his making a difference in our lives. It is true that God changes all he touches. Is this just church rhetoric? Does it really happen?

Indeed it does! There is a mighty force within God to change those who come into contact with their Maker.

But we can expect something else from grace, from this Manufacturer's product: compassionate understanding. Sometimes just by being touched by the Maker, we can understand better how all of life is assembled. The church often walks past the wounded of this world. This blasé lack of concern does not flatter God. However, when the Manufacturer's product parts are assembled, compassionate understanding walks *toward* the wounded, offering this new product with a kind warmth.

One other quality we can expect from this product is courage. People who have been touched by their Maker find the strength of purpose to do things that they would never have believed themselves capable of doing. Yet why are such achievements so impressive to weak humans? Don't we know that having faith that God will work miracles is only a reasonable expectation of the manufacturer of miracles?

I teach in a theological seminary. Many missionaries come to my classes on their furloughs to learn from me

126

things I never feel adequate to teach them. In fact, although they never seem to see it within themselves, I see them as men and women of extraordinary power. "Ordinary miracles" are their way of life. The power of their accomplishments cannot be explained outside of the power of Christ. They walk into hostile villages and peace becomes the order of the day. At times they preach and teach under civil threat, seeing nothing of the heroic in their workaday lives.

Nonetheless, they are heroic. Their unseen triumphs have their roots in the words of Joshua: "Have not I commanded thee? Be strong and of good courage; be not afraid, neither be thou dismayed: for the LORD thy God is with thee withersoever thou goest" (KJV). No wonder the psalmist could say, "Even though I walk through the valley of the shadow of death, I will fear no evil." Or again:

> He is my refuge and my fortress, my God, in whom I trust. Surely he will save you from the fowler's snare and from the deadly pestilence. He will cover you with his feathers, and under his wings you will find refuge; his faithfulness will be your shield and rampart. You will not fear the terror of night, nor the arrow that flies by day, nor the pestilence that stalks in the darkness, nor the plague that destroys at midday. A thousand may fall at your side and ten thousand at your right hand, but it will not come near you. . . . For he will command his angels concerning you to guard you in all your ways; they will lift you up in their hands so that you will not strike your foot against a stone. You will tread the lion and the cobra.

Extraordinary courage is the child born of grace.

The people of God do not always win, but they never lose alone. I think that the greatest part of the Manufacturer's warranty is that he promises that you will never have to take one step of your life unaccompanied. He is always there! In his unceasing presence there is the power to face whatever you must. Perhaps this last quality of the product encompasses all.

In his presence is grace.

In his presence is change.

In his presence is courage.

In his presence is relationship.

Of Blindness and Light

There is no doubt that Jesus is the Great Physician. But he is a specialist in all fields: I have experienced his renovation work on my entire values system, and I know him for a heart surgeon. After he healed my heart, he touched my eyes with new vision, and I saw him as an eye surgeon.

"A scalpel, Nurse, and steady now;
Your fingers must not show their fright.
My knife must cut away the dark—
Restore the blessed hope of light.

"Adjust the clamp; I need more room;
Mop the water from my brow.
More anesthetic, Orderly;
Prepare the sterile forceps now."

The Doctor's hand clasps sure the blade.
His wrists are firm; his fingers ply
A steady, "delicado" hope,
And lay the lancet on the eye.

"None at all stand near me, please,
To jar my hand or touch the bed.
Even interns, please step back,
And leave me room about the head."

The lancet makes the feather cut;
Syringes draw the red aside;
The forceps lift the cataract
And lay it on the culture slide.

O blessed is the Surgeon
Who ends this endless night
By bandaging the blinded
To restore them to their sight!

Even so the Great Physician
Cuts away the blinding part,
Lifts your soul to see his love,
Turns the light on in your heart!

THE NIGHT THE SIDESHOW WAS BOUGHT

Freaks are souls in search of image. Conversion is a mirror Christ furnishes for a new look at ourselves.

Myron/Myra, the hermaphrodite, was confused about who he/she was. All the others in the freak show were also confused about themselves. Iva Gillette, the bearded lady, admitted from the very day she joined the circus that she had been unable to see herself as anything other than a freak. The word *freak* bothered Myron/Myra as much as it did Iva Gillette. Philip-Fido, the dog-faced boy, agreed. So did Thumbelina and the Fat Man.

The whole crew had been drawn into a common need for each other by terribly low self-esteem and the fact that they had sold themselves to be the slaves of a tyrannical owner. They were the ugly and the damned, making a life out of being too fat or too little or too deformed. They had all endured years of being gawked at, laughed at, ogled, and despised.

None of them will ever forget the Thursday when their world seemed to perish. It was Thumbelina whose tiny voice broke into their odd gathering: "The circus is sold!"

"Who owns us now?" asked Philip-Fido.

"What difference does it make? We're all a bunch of freaks!" The Fat Man, consumed with self-pity, began to shake all over with sobs. His immense body rolled like a mountain under siege of a grievous earthquake. "Freaks, freaks, freaks . . ." His voice trailed off.

Iva Gillette stroked her beard, then shook her head and sat, silent.

"Who owns us now?" Again, Philip-Fido asked the same question.

"I bought the circus," said a voice belonging to the new owner, who had walked suddenly into their conversation.

The new owner seemed kind, and the bearded lady smiled. "I was afraid our new owner would be just like the last one." Iva Gillette, like the Fat Man, began to weep. "I wish my beard was pulled out."

"Mine was once," said the new owner.

"Who are you, and what do you know of being glowered at, laughed at, pointed at?" asked Myron/Myra. "Our last owner forced me to take off all my clothes every night so the ticket holders could laugh at me."

"I was once naked and laughed at," said the new owner.

They sat, silent.

"I bought this sideshow so I could set you free," said the owner. "I bought you—all of you are free."

"Free?" said Thumbelina in tiny-voiced contempt. "You are tall; I am small," said Thumbelina. "I don't want to hear anyone tall tell me of freedom!"

"*Small* is but a state of heart that afflicts those who have accepted too much of this world's harsh opinion. *Tall* is getting the true view of yourself. Trust me, you can be free. Indeed, you shall be free!"

"Free?" sneered the Fat Man.

"Free?" laughed Myron/Myra.

The new owner walked over to the Fat Man and handed him a mirror. "Look in this glass, and you will see yourself for the first time." The Fat Man looked. His face stole into a smile. He didn't see fat—he saw virtue, loyalty, human kindness, and a spontaneous sense of humor.

132

Suddenly his obesity seemed trivial and unworthy of its dehumanizing force.

The new owner drew a second mirror from inside his jacket and handed it to Thumbelina. She, too, gazed fondly into the glass and smiled. "Leave off the 'Thumbe;' I'm 'Lina' now!"

He drew a third mirror and held it out to Philip-Fido, and his "dog face" was suddenly alive with light.

"And, which will it be—Myron or Myra?" asked the owner as he handed out yet another glass.

"Well, I've always liked baseball better than soap operas . . . ," he/she faltered.

"Very well, Myron!" said the owner.

Instantly, Myron ordered Myra back to her daytime television, and she was gone forever. Myron felt like a quarterback after a Rose Bowl touchdown.

Five very normal people, at last, watched as the owner walked away. Near the end of the sideshow tent, he turned, took a Bic lighter, and flicked the flint wheel. Fire jumped from the wick, and he touched it to the canvas tent. He smiled. Amber canvas roared orange against the night.

THE MIDNIGHT KNOCK AT THE DOOR

I offer this poem to those children who presently have little courage, along with this rule: Never answer the door if anyone else will.

You can't be too careful near midnight
If you hear a knock at your door.
Some folks are welcome to come right on inside,
And others you ought to ignore.

If, in the dark, you see two big kind eyes
And a woman standing alone:
It could be the lovely and sweet Avon lady,
Moonlighting to sell her cologne.

If the eyes that you see are wearing a mask
That is covered all over with stars,
It could be the Opera Phantom—or worse—
So, ask him to sing a few bars.

It's thoroughly safe if two pairs of eyes
Appear right on top of the other,
Just say, "Please come in!" You'll find it quite safe.
It's a kangaroo kid and his mother.

But if you should see a single, wide eye,
It could be the Cyclops Adolphus;
So slam the door loud and yell in the dark,
"I already gave at the office!"

But if you see two very big bloodshot eyes,
No Girl Scout is selling cookies for fun.
Just say, "Stay right there;" then dash to the phone
And quickly dial nine-one-one.

But the smartest thing to be done
With a midnight knock at your door
Is yell down the hall to your father,
And say, "Dad, please get the door!"

THE YOKE

I appreciate those friends who have stood by me in a crisis, when my standing alone would have been impossible. I have some friends for whom I would do that.

I will not have you walk this monstrous path
Alone. The gargoyles lurk and offer all
The bubbling cup of fact distilled in wrath—
Sweet mingled hemlock: vinegar and gall.
The dingy halls hold death. You cannot see
The cobwebbed glory of old fishermen
And martyrs' skulls—bone-crushed divinity
In alabaster vials of Magdalene.

Long gone—there's where the dream is lost and won.
The frigid air around your little fray
Will thaw on bloody wood in God's warm sun,
Where scholars crucify the souls who pray.

    With feet unscarred I'll walk with you, my friend,
    Though both of us be crucified again.

THE NEAR GOD

*The faith of Brother Lawrence often eludes me: washing
dishes in a monastery while honoring the Mass. Like
him, I seek to remain at worship while my hands stay
busy with the business of serving others.*

In search of God, I often pry
His ordered universe apart;
And learn that when my quest is done,
I find him in my very heart.

Red Book, Blue Book

Scarlett Redding was a reader. She was what her church called "a red-book reader." The books she read came mostly from the church near her home; those books that weren't from her church, were church approved. Now Scarlett was not just any old reader: she was a reader in search of excellence. Scarlett knew that excellence was somehow tied to the reading of books—*good books* (what her church called "red books")—and so she read. Indeed, she read regularly, only stopping to change books or replace the bulb in her desk lamp. Though she was born into the age of books, she had not yet read all of the books there were. And all books she read were as red in color as the blushing librarians who collected her overdue fines.

It was odd. There was no law that said that all books *had* to be red in color, that's just the way it was. So, if you were a reader, all of your reading was done from red books. They were not all the same shade of red: some were catsup red; some were rose red; some were Tabasco colored; others were a strawberry-popsicle shade. There were light red books and deep red books. Books to be taken seriously were crimson. And books that didn't need to be taken so seriously were barely pink. While she never bragged that she could tell a book by its cover color, she had handled so many of them that she had only to see the redness of a book to guess the quality of its content.

Even Scarlett's little room was ringed with red, as bookcases lined the room. Her room was nearly as red as the inside of a bookstore, which was the reddest place on earth.

But Scarlett began to find that as she grew older, red no longer intrigued her. Red went dead for Scarlett. She found herself becoming disconsolate. Pink, cerise, and crimson all spelled out *b-o-r-e*. No matter how red the books were, they were colorless to Scarlett. At first she held on to the brightest and reddest books, but soon all the reds became the absence of color for Scarlett. And though she didn't throw away the books in her room, she quit reading them altogether. When she passed the red windows of bookstores, she always looked the other way.

The colorless, bookless months passed Scarlett by.

One day as Scarlett passed a bookstore, an old man extended his hand to her and beckoned her inside. She followed. The red interior was so red that it gave her hot flashes as she passed boring shelf after boring shelf and headed to the back room. In the room at the back of the store, the old man handed her a plain brown bag and told her not to open it until she was safely at home. She obeyed.

As she made her way through the store, suddenly Scarlett froze. Maybe the old man was a member of the Society for Utmost Preservation of Excellence in Reading Betterment—an intellectual—her mother had always told her to avoid intellectuals with brown bags. She hurried out of the store and, clutching her little brown bag, ran through the streets. She could not imagine what was in the bag, but she guarded it as though some lurking fiend might leap out from behind a shrub and forcibly tear it away.

At last she arrived home. Eagerly her hands tore away the paper sack, and there greeting her was a most wonderful sight: a *blue* book! What an odd thing. She felt as though she were doing something terribly wrong, just holding a book so blue. *I'll bet he was a liberal intellectual,* thought Scarlett. *No sincere church member would read a blue book.* Still, she could not be critical for long. The blue of the book hypnotized her. It was banner blue, and robin's-egg blue; it was jay blue and sea blue and star blue; it was a frothy-waterfall-in-summer blue; it was a lying-flat-on-the-grass-and-looking-up-at-the-sky-all-alone-in-July blue.

Scarlett clutched the book to her bosom and looked around. The red books in her room seemed to glare in disapproval. So she turned her back on the glaring, haughty books and flexed the bright blue cover of her new book in her fingers nervously. Cautious and trembling, she opened the cover. On the first page in rainbow letters she read, "A Truly Excellent Book."

What would a truly excellent book contain? wondered Scarlett as she turned to the table of contents. She was surprised that there were only three chapters in the blue book. The first chapter was called "God Is All Over." The second chapter's title was "God Has a Boy Just like Us." And the third chapter was "The World Is Wide and There Are Many Kinds of Truth." It also had a very long subtitle: "There Are Biblical Truths, but Also Scientific Truths and Mathematical Truths and Historical Truths, Some of Which Are Not Mentioned in the Bible." There was nothing like this in the red books.

Scarlett turned to chapter one, and when she rubbed her finger over the words *God Is All Over,* she felt altogether weak with wonder, for no sooner had her finger touched the word *God* than her eyes beheld a thousand scenes of stars and galaxies and lands. There were colliding sun systems that kept exploding so that Scarlett was struck silent by the laser majesty that ripped her room with light.

"Oh, this is an excellent book," she said. "Never did I

know that God is all over till right now."

She turned to chapter two: "God Has a Boy Just like Us." That was the very best chapter she ever read, for never did she see the wonder of being alive until that moment. She saw God's Boy! He seemed kind and patient and was very strong. God's Boy was just like God. "God's Boy *is* God's show-and-tell," said Scarlett half aloud. "Still, he's not only like God, he's like me, too!" She could tell just by looking at him that there was nothing that he couldn't do, and yet he was just like her. It made her feel good to know that God had a Boy just like her, for she knew that God's Boy understood just how good it felt to feel good and how bad it felt to feel bad.

Maybe some intellectuals aren't so bad, thought Scarlett. Then she read the title of chapter three.

It was the third chapter that gave her so much trouble. It didn't seem related to the first and second chapters. She thought and thought about the third chapter: "The World Is Wide and There Are Many Kinds of Truth." She thought about all the kinds of truth that didn't seem very related to God at all. She thought of trigonometry and microwave makers and cosmetology and peanut-butter factories; she thought of silver nitrate and cave paintings and submarines and curling irons and suspension bridges and malt balls and tenant farmers and astronauts and leg warmers and George Washington—all true things. How did all of these kinds of truth relate? She simply couldn't understand. *Yes, there are many kinds of truth that don't seem related to Bible truths at all,* she thought.

This book on excellence is hard. To be excellent you have to think too hard, she thought. *The World Is Wide and There Are Many Kinds of Truth.* Scarlett kept thinking about the last chapter until at last she fell sound asleep.

In the morning, the very first thing that Scarlett reached for was her new blue book. She read once more. When she came again to the troublesome third chapter, no matter how hard she tried, she just couldn't make the third chapter relate. It made her very sad. *Intellectual blue—that's what this book is,* she thought. *I shouldn't read blue books; they only confuse me, for there is too much truth in the world. . . . No, that's absurd. There could never be too much truth, only too many lies.*

As Scarlett got dressed for the day, she had an idea. She walked down Third Street to Main Street, past her church to the public library.

The library had always been there, right next to the church, but Scarlett rarely went there. The truth is that red-church people hardly had time for libraries. They were at church a lot. There were glow-red revival and reeking-red renewal weekends. There were prayer services and Revelation studies. There were film series, red-red committee alerts, and program-planning sessions for all the red meetings. So the red people hardly had time for libraries; in fact, they discouraged them.

But now Scarlett walked into the library and saw that the entire building was filled with books. Just as she expected, the books there were mostly various shades of red, except that here and there was a blue book. The blue books seemed like they were all friends even though they were usually a long way apart on the shelves.

The world really is big, thought Scarlett, *and there are many kinds of truth.* Scarlett turned down an aisle between huge ranks of books. They were on shelves and stretched up so high above her, she had to get a ladder to reach the top. She got a big ladder and shoved it to the top of a section called "Anatomy." Scarlett climbed all the way to the top, and there she pulled out a little blue book; it was titled *Human Anatomy*.

She opened the book. On one of the pages was a picture of a skeleton. "I must have a skeleton inside of me, too!" said Scarlett, and then it occurred to her that if God's Boy was just like her, *he* must have had a skeleton inside him, too. On the skeleton's leg was a word that read *femur. I have a femur,* thought Scarlett, *and I guess if I have one, God's Boy must have had a femur, too.* It made her feel silly thinking about Jesus' femur, but she was sure it must be true.

She thumbed on through the pages till she saw another picture of a man with his skin gone away. The man was all muscles, and each of his muscles was labeled with little black lines that ran from his muscles out to a big, long word. She saw one muscle called *biceps femoris*. She said the words out loud: "bi-c-e-p-s f-e-moris"—Scarlett found that difficult words had to be sounded out loud to be pronounced. Some people who were in the library shushed her, since they did not like hearing anyone say "biceps femoris" out loud in the library.

Hmm, I must have biceps femoris too . . . and so did God's Boy. These are two truths. The world is wide, and all truth is from God. Suddenly she could see that God was all through the library.

All day long she stayed in the library. She read a book about mushrooms and could see that God's truth was all through the book: even those people who cultivated mushrooms were like God's Boy.

"That's funny," said Scarlett, "even books that ignore God have some truth in them." She felt sorry for people who didn't believe in God, but it made her feel very good that their books had truths in them.

Truth doesn't have to use the word God *to be friends with God,* she thought.

At the top of one of the shelves, Scarlett saw a book with the title *Gravity.* It was a book that told the truth about how nobody could just float up and away and off the earth. Scarlett was happy for that truth. For gravity held her to the floor of the library. It also once held God's Boy to the ground. Scarlett could barely make good *gravy,* so she was grateful that God could make something as wonderful as *gravity. It's just like God to keep our feet flat on the ground while we learn all about him,* thought Scarlett.

When Scarlett went home that night, she saw for the first time that there was much to be found that was alike between all three chapters of her new blue book. She loved it. She read it every day and every night. And every new thing that Scarlett heard, she tried to think, *Is this the truth? How is it related to "There Are Many Kinds of Truth" and "God Has a Boy Just like Us"?*

Sunday came, and Scarlett went to church. Scarlett just loved her little church, for they always had a place right at the very end of the service where you could tell something wonderful and glorious that you had learned that week. It was called "Wonderful and Glorious Time." Scarlett could hardly wait to tell that she had learned that the world is very large and all truth is from God and all true truth relates to God and his Boy. The preacher preached a wonderful sermon entitled "God Is All Over." Scarlett thought of her new blue book and was very happy. When the preacher finished, the choir sang a glorious anthem called "God Has a Boy Just like Us." Scarlett smiled.

When the choir was finished, it was Wonderful and Glorious Time, and the preacher asked if anyone had learned anything new that week.

144

"Yes," cried Scarlett, "I learned that the world is wide and there are many kinds of truth and all truth relates to God and his Boy."

Everyone looked very embarrassed. Finally the preacher cleared his throat and said, "Is this fact related to 'God is all over'? You know how we feel here; it must be related."

"Yes, I think so. For the more I read at the library—"

An old woman in the choir stiffened. "The library? Humph!" She cupped her hand over her mouth and whispered to a bony-faced man beside her, "You can learn some *bad* truths in the library."

"Oh, no!" cried Scarlett. "There are no bad truths. That's another thing I've learned this week. All truths are the friends of God."

"Why didn't you come to the all-red revival and renewal retreat?" rasped the old woman. "If you want to live a red and righteous life, you must keep away from blue books."

One man gasped. He had never heard anyone say "blue books" right in church! "Is that all you learned this week: that the world is wide and that all truths are the friends of God?"

"Oh, no!" cried Scarlett. "I learned that Jesus had a femur and a biceps femoris."

Now everybody gasped.

". . . And besides that, people who plant mushrooms are just like Jesus, and gravity held Jesus to the ground. We're all floaters without it! And it's hard to learn any kind of truth when you're floating around."

"Enough!" they cried. Just then someone noticed that Scarlett was carrying a blue book. A strong elder tore it from her hand and took it to the pastor. "Burn it!" he cried.

"Please, no!" cried Scarlett. But they took the book away and Scarlett left, crying all the way home. Could she have

145

been mistaken? Is the world wide? Are all truths of God? She thought about it all night. When morning came, she got up and got dressed and decided that she would give up books and church forever. *Did God have a boy just like us?* Scarlett was confused. *Is God all over?* she puzzled. She knew that it was true, and yet she knew that she must not anger people by ever again suggesting that the world was big and that all truths were from God.

She shuffled along the sidewalks going nowhere in particular, when she saw an old man with a brown sack under his arm. *Oh!* she thought. *It's that same wonderful intellectual who gave me the blue book.* She hid behind a row of shrubs, and the old man sauntered past her. He was mumbling something. She listened very carefully but could hear nothing. She began to feel guilty for eavesdropping. He was old, and she hated to hear him talking to himself.

She had an inclination to follow him. Quickly, Scarlett stepped behind the old man and trailed along after him. He never saw her, but she kept her eyes on him and particularly the brown sack he carried. She thought she knew what was in it. But try as she might, she couldn't figure out what the old man way saying.

At last the old man turned into a shady lane and walked down a path through the row of trees. There was a little white house at the side of the road. On the door of the little white house was a sign: "Enter Here with a Word of Truth." The old man turned up to the door and raised the brass lion's head that was the door knocker. He rapped three times, and the door opened just a little. Someone on the inside said, "The password, please!"

"The world is wide and all truth is from God," said the old man, but he said it too softly for Scarlett to hear.

How Scarlett wished she could have heard his reply.

Once he was inside, she knew that she had to get into that little house, too. Quickly, she ran up to the door and knocked with the great lion's-head knocker three times. The door creaked open only a little on its hinges. "Yes?" said a throaty voice.

"May I come in?" asked Scarlett.

"You may enter with a word of truth," said someone inside.

I wonder what kind of truth he wants, thought Scarlett. She knew she would have to guess. "Mount Everest is the highest mountain on earth."

The door slammed. Scarlett rapped again.

Again the door creaked open and the man inside insisted this time, "You may enter only with a word of truth."

Scarlett was desperate. "Jupiter is the largest planet in the solar system," she blurted.

Again the door slammed shut.

Scarlett was confused. Maybe just any old truth wasn't good enough for the doorkeeper. Maybe the password should try to relate truths of all kinds to certain specific truths. It was worth a try, so she rapped the lion's head a third time.

The door swung open an inch or so.

"Password, please," said the throaty voice.

"Jesus had a femur and a biceps femoris." Scarlett felt ashamed—there were so many truths, but she couldn't think of one great enough to impress the doorkeeper. She fully expected the door to slam shut.

"Well, it isn't exactly the truth we were looking for," he said, "but it is a truth that does relate to the fact that God is all over and God had a Boy. I guess we'll have to let you in. Have you ever read a blue book?"

"I had one once, but it got taken from me in church."

"During Wonderful and Glorious Time?" asked the door-keeper.

Scarlett was amazed. Even as her mouth dropped open, she entered the room. It was filled with many people, and all of them had blue books. There were paper sacks all over the floor.

"Do you love God?" they asked Scarlett.

"Oh yes!" said Scarlett.

"Do you believe he is all over?"

"Not only all over, but all over all over!"

Scarlett felt that she was overdoing it now.

"Do you believe he had a Boy just like us?"

"Oh yes: not only just like us, but just like all the people who only read red books or no books at all. His Boy was like every person that ever lived: like the men and like the little children and like the poor people who starve to death and like scientists who sometimes teach things we don't believe and like people from Indiana and astronauts and—"

The man who had asked the question cleared his throat.

"Do you truly believe that Jesus was God's Boy and had a femur and a biceps femoris? Are you willing to take a stand for all truth—even during Wonderful and Glorious Time?"

"Oh yes, sir, for the world is big and all truth is from God."

"Then you are welcome to the Society for Utmost Pres-ervation of Excellence in Reading Betterment."

A little man advanced from the side and handed her a blue book.

"Treasure this book," he said, "for such books are owned by those who really care about true excellence."

"Are there many alive right now in our world who care about excellence?" asked Scarlett.

"There have never been many who care about excellence," said the little man. "But numbers don't matter, my dear Scarlett; only excellence matters."

"Now," he said, "let us all take out our books."

And they all did. First they turned to chapter one. They all felt the words "God Is All Over," and the room darkened and a bright light traveled in an orbit around a growing universe. It was wonderful and glorious, but Scarlett knew it was even wider and better than that.

Then they turned to chapter two and felt the words "God Has a Boy Just like Us." As they rubbed the words, the great light in the center of the center of the universe condensed down and became a man—a man, Scarlett could see, who had been maltreated. She couldn't see a book in the man's hand, but it was almost as though they had torn a blue book away from him and then nailed him on a tree. He cried out some words. Scarlett couldn't tell what the words were, but it must have sounded like the password, for the heavens opened a little way, and then soon he was dead. But then he was alive again! Scarlett saw a wonderful thing. God's Boy began to rise off a mountain top, and he floated upward. *Books on gravity teach that rising upward is impossible,* remembered Scarlett. *Oh well, I guess if God makes gravity, he can unmake it whenever he wants to.*

Soon the meeting was over, and all the people put their blue books back into their sacks and left the quiet little house of wonders. Scarlett walked home alone past the library and smiled at all the truth it contained. Then she walked past the church and thought of all the truth it contained. And she clutched her little paper sack and knew that libraries and churches didn't have to be afraid of each other ever again. Inside of her, she was glad. She thought of Jesus and smiled. Wasn't it like him to love intellectuals who read blue books and red-church people and ordinary mushroom pickers who needed gravity to keep hanging around? "Thank you, Jesus, for being just like us," she said out loud. She hopped off the ground and tried to imagine how Jesus felt that day he made gravity look silly. It was a beautiful day. She felt good—all the way down to her femur and her biceps femoris.

ECCE HOMO II

Journal entry, September 8, 1978

Jesus! What have I done? My God, dear friend!
The gnats have gathered at your swollen eyes.
Your lips can no longer speak to defend
Your innocence. You breathe the final sighs
Of life. You can't stop dying to begin again.
I know the tale. I know that you will rise.
But I am ripped to see your hands so pinned
And covered with a swelling clot of flies.

I kiss your cross. Forgive me here. I've grown
Too weak to roll back Sunday morning's stone.
Insanity now screams my obscene loss.
You workers, here—raise up another cross!

   One cross away—you'll hear my timid moan,
   Dear Christ. Repentance offered in a groan.

VI. Whistling While You Work on Christmas Eve

VI. WHISTLING WHILE YOU WORK ON CHRISTMAS EVE

Whistling While You Work on Christmas Eve

Perhaps because it comes at the end of the year, Christmas is a time when I tend to put so much of life together. It's not just the things that go under the tree. At Christmas I am prone to repair old relationships and broken promises. I am more pensive about ill-fitting moods and careless remembrances. So I always get a bit mystical at Christmas. And at this beautiful season of the year, I emphasize within myself the real and enduring values I have frequently hurried past during earlier times of the year.

For some, the season of the Incarnation is a time when revelry turns to drunkenness and suicide is more frequent than at any other time of the year. But perhaps this is so because most of the human race is trying to assemble its own ill-fitting priorities on Christmas Eve.

The anticipation of earlier Christmas Eves has always been complicated by my "fatherly" need to put something together in order to delight my children. One Christmas this need required me to assemble a Radio Flyer wagon. Another Yuletide, it was a dollhouse. Another time, an electric train. Under the uncertain lights of Christmas Eve, I was always racing to get something assembled and so furnish my children with grand surprises.

Somehow that's what Calvary and Easter Sunday seem to me to be about. God has always been putting human redemption together, assembling the complex parts of history and human need so that he could give to us the grandest present of all.

Along with the apostle Paul, I respond, "Thanks be to God for his indescribable gift."

A Shepherd's Testimony

In December of 1992 a group of students was putting on a mini-pageant for our seminary. One of them asked me why it was that the shepherds never got any good lines in Christmas pageants. I reminded him that shepherds were part of the working class but that the kings were the wealthy sponsors of the Nativity. But after I thought it over, I decided that here and there, at least in some pageants, it would be all right for the shepherds to get some time. So I wrote this to give shepherds a place in the program. After all, Nativity stories should be places where even the blue-collared folks get their turn.—Christmas 1992

It was just after midnight when the gold broke all around us! The light stung my eyes. It was the worst I've ever felt, I tell you. I choke and gagged. I don't know why—I must have been allergic to all that light. I was terrified. These big, silvery white beings belched out of the skies, like a tangled flock of big geese. Tall as Mount Hermon and big as Philistines. Those bright, big fellows exploded out of the shattered blackness and fell like the sparks from the blacksmith's forge all around our feet.

The sheep whelped like wolf cubs and hid their little black faces in each other's fleeces. I turned to see how my fellow shepherds were doing. My friend Ben was worse off than me: he was laying on the ground in a stone-cold faint. Judah was still conscious, but he had his face hidden in his sleeve, muttering, "No . . . no . . . no!" My skin started to crawl. My eyes twitched. The hair on my neck prickled and then tried to crawl down my collar.

Name any fear I've ever felt before this, and I'll deny the force of it. I never in all my life was afraid till that night. The angels did it all. They burst upon me, forcing me into sheer terror of that much splendor at midnight. It was like the dark nightmares you have as a child, but it was a nightmare with all light. I saw everything, and I trembled.

"Fear not!" said one of the big fellows. (His message was half-a-coronary too late for Ben.) "I bring you good news! A baby's been born. 'This day in the city of David, a Savior. . . . And this shall be a sign unto you, you shall find the baby wrapped in clean cloths and lying in a manger.' "

This, I assume, was the way angels asked you to set out looking for stuff.

The light was still eye-painful and bright, but I didn't have the nerve to say, "Please call off this light, would you?" All of a sudden the whole flock—or whatever you call a group of angels—started singing, "Glory to God in the highest and on earth, peace to men of good will!"

Then they were gone, just like that! When all that light and noise was over, things got dark and quiet. The dark was so dark you couldn't see your hand in front of your face.

"You still there, Judah?" I whispered, still recovering from the whole thing. No answer.

"Judah," I spoke a little louder now, "are you there?"

"For pity's sake, be quiet. They might come back!" he said.

"Think we ought to do what they said and go look for the baby? Can we leave the sheep out here without one of us?"

158

"They're not going anywhere; they're too paralyzed to move."

About this time Ben regained consciousness and, after we explained everything about the light and the angels and the whole chorus, the three of us started off toward Bethlehem.

Our legs were all goose bumps during the first mile of our walk into Bethlehem. And we got off to a slow start because our knees were knocking. But gradually we settled into a faster pace. We found the tiny baby and his folks just like the angels said. I don't know why this surprised us. There they were, and the baby was wrapped in clean cloths and lying in a manger.

We didn't feel too comfortable barging in on the little family. And even though there was something kingly and queenly about the mother and father, they weren't dressed much better than Ben, Judah, or me. But it seemed the right thing to do, somehow, just falling on our knees.

We didn't know what to say to the new parents. Judah said, "Congratulations on your new kid; the angels told us about him." Then Ben said, "You must have been pregnant a long time." It was the stupidest thing I ever heard anybody say. Judah elbowed him in the ribs for being so mutton-headed. Ben hardly ever left the sheep, so he never had developed much in the way of social graces; I guess it seemed logical to him.

The woman just smiled, to let him know he could be an idiot if he liked. I kind of glossed the whole thing over by saying, "There must be something real special about your little baby, if angels are having a big party for him in the fields at night."

Long after we got up off our knees and went back to the sheep, I kept thinking about that evening. I never will forget two things about that night: I'll never forget Ben's stupidity, and I'll never forget how beautiful that couple looked. They were peasants, I guess. Still, I've never quit wondering who they were and who their baby grew up to be. And one other thing I've never gotten over: I just never have trusted the dark again. Ever since that night, I get a little edgy around midnight.

*Two hitchhikers changed our church, Christmastime
1989. What they taught us was that we feel pity for the
couple in Bethlehem who were homeless long ago, but
fail to offer the same sympathy to other common, yet
"holy," families in our circle of ministry. I, for one, will
long be grateful for the hitchhikers' lesson.*

On our 30th wedding anniversary, I took my wife's old
engagement ring to a jeweler and had him lift the diamond
from its modest company of jewels and set it down in a
new cluster of outrageous sparkle. The result was exquisite.

Although something of great value, that diamond, after
30 years, had quit speaking—precisely because it had spoken for so long in the same way. Now its new enhancement
caused it to proclaim the older covenants with a glistening
new vigor. Something old and precious received new voice
by being set in a newer context.

A similar recasting is often necessary at Christmas. Fa-
miliarity breeds a dull Noel. Because there are only a few
Scripture passages that describe the Christmas story, each
December we may hear all of them four and five times.
We enter Yuletide with yawns, perhaps envying the shep-
herds who heard the *first* rendition of "Peace on earth."
But what woke them in joy, puts us to sleep.

We find ourselves in love with the season but dulled by
its ever-cycling familiarity. If the story is so wonderful,
why so often doesn't it seem that way?

A few years ago around Christmastime, a sharply dressed

businessman from our church was crossing our state on I-80, that 450-mile stretch of highway that bisects Nebraska west from east. Somewhere west of Omaha, he passed a couple hitchhiking. They were obviously poor. The woman looked very cold—and very pregnant.

My friend picked them up and brought them to Omaha. With the help of others, he arranged for their housing. About a month later, the child was born.

Just before the baby's birth, I was invited to a dinner at an elegant home in honor of the rescued couple. They were rustic and a bit uncouth. The woman, now great with child, often belched embarrassingly loudly during the festive affair. The upper-middle-class guests looked greatly chagrined.

I must confess that I, too, felt an unspoken sternness as I beheld the couple. I did not immediately liken them to the couple from Luke 2. But later I did wonder, if I had been running a Holiday Inn in Bethlehem, whether I would have asked them to please stay at the Best Western . . . or offered them the barn out back. Especially if the woman had told me that their Blue Cross insurance had expired and she was having labor pains!

Every time I now hear the Christmas story, I think about this couple. I don't like the similarities I see between myself and the innkeeper in Bethlehem that first-century night when a couple of hitchhikers were in trouble. But I do know that the Christmas story will never be quite the same for me again. This homeless couple has placed the wonderful drama of the first Christmas in a new setting. Now Bethlehem has been reborn in the redeeming glitter it deserves. A whole—entirely middle class—church congregation has been tutored by a family, who became for us more of a holy family than they suspected.

162

LOVE NEVER FAILED

A past Christmas—the date of the composition is lost to me.

I cried when first I read about his death,
For God's extremity was lavish love
Flung manward—until none of hate was left.
Divinity had taken off his gloves
To meet my naked hand in his, and then
The ugliness of self-indulgence died;
The King laid by his crown to be my friend:
Eternity and time slept side by side.

Dear God, can every Christmas day of joy be
The evidence you planned it all with me
In mind? The silhouette of grace hand-nailed
Upon rough, weathered wood has never failed.

   He loved us till his breathing died,
   And distant suns withheld their light and cried.

LOVE STORY

Journal entry, Christmas 1979

She waits while over there he knocks. Again
Refused! Nor is there place throughout the town.
Be strong as steel, lest Joseph sense the pain
You feel. It's yet a while till you lay down
To sleep. "There's nowhere else to go tonight,"
He said. She fought the burning in her eyes:
Rebuked her tears before they fell. Starlight
Crowned the cold, small town with fiery skies.

He took her in his arms and that embrace
Dissolved the desperation that they faced.
"I paid the stable rent," he said with shame.
"Your son will come tonight." One kiss she gave.

Joy blessed the silent night! Salvation came—
An infant whimper from the shepherd's cave.

THEY SAY IT NEVER SNOWS IN BETHLEHEM

Fall 1981

They say it never snows in Bethlehem!
I do not chide that warmer place he chose
To make himself a man. Still Jesse's stem
Was never sheathed in ice. Nor did the snows
Impede the Magis' camels or the frost
Glisten on the shepherds' crooks. The flight
Of Gabriel was straight. No gales were crossed;
No blizzards bound this courier of light.

These frosted festive plains know better joy—
Wind—sculptured drifts—sun brilliant, silvered, grand—
Might better light the eyes of Mary's boy.
I wish his eyes has seen this ice-bright land.

    For snow can sanctify a holy night
    With jeweled elegance and formal white.

REPUTATION

Christmas 1986

"Scandal! Shame!" the village gossips cried.
"A sullied maid of seventeen!" Below
Contempt, she laid her self-esteem aside—
Reached up and begged the skies to hear, as though
The stars would trust what mortal minds denied.
Exiled from all but God, she seemed to know
That none would ever call her heaven's bride—
No one would see her child as heaven's son.

God was her tutor on how kings must come
To waiting, doubting orbs where maids retreat
Before those skeptics would ban God's Son
From any womb where earth and heaven might meet.

 Yet, seventeen are years enough to see
 That meaning treads on seas of mystery.

The Season of Hope

Christmas 1985

Come! Isn't this the season of his birth?
The air is brittle-crisp. The frost and glow
Are back, whitewashing melancholy earth.
This winterscape of carols set in snow
Are anthems sung to praise the infant grand.
But why this one? This same day quite alone,
Ten thousand babies marked the cruel land
With seas of graves where his bright star once shone.

The world is cold this Christmas Eve. The oil
Is nearly gone. We've glutted year by year
Upon his great resources. And we toil
With fears the infant does not seem to cheer.

Yet in this cradled straw, grace can reside
And we have hope, because a baby cried.

DIVINE APPOINTMENT

Christmas 1984

This little foot! Can we ever know where,
Grown stronger, it shall walk? A ragged girl
Now holds her baby close. The barnyard air
Is stirred by alien wings, and light is hurled
Across the midnight fields to startle sheep.
While thunder deafens shepherds, fiery flame
Ignites the skies with infant footprints, deep
In space, to trace his cosmic, saving name.

Poor vagrant mother, count your joys as thieves.
Your little boy must grow to feel and bleed.
The universe already sees and grieves.
Your nursing martyr and his coming need.

This tiny foot that walked through stars above,
Must yet wade pain to keep a date with love.

DECEMBER THAW

Christmas 1976

Poor frozen world, all ice within, without.
Your icy worldviews are frozen, too.
Why be so deaf to that great shout
Of life that pierced the planet's gloom? Do you
Yet rise to mock the stable with your doubt
That Mary's child is somehow not the new
And prior evidence that you have hope,
Within the darkness where you blindly grope?

Stop doubting, please, and see this Jewish boy.
He tore the barrier of thick dead skies
To love you to the limits of his joy—
And you are healed by his faint infant's cry.

   Please stand, love-blinded at a cosmic rift,
   Heart-hushed by his unspeakable, great gift.

Once upon a time there was a little town called Pleasantville. This town was not a grand tourist attraction; in fact, it was such a quiet place that it rarely made the news. Because it was not on the main road, nobody ever went *through* it except those who were going *to* it.

The town had a shiny new town hall of which it was justifiably proud. And in the shiny new town hall was the grand mayor of Pleasantville. On occasions of state, he had even been called "The Lord High Mayor of Pleasantville." This delighted him, for he was extremely proud of his title, and the town was no less proud of its mayor.

The pride was not unwarranted on the part of the townsmen, for most agreed that he had done far more for Pleasantville than any other mayor in the history of the city. Not only had he been responsible for the erection of the new city hall, but also for the donation of a granite drinking fountain and a public playground.

One day when the town council convened, the exchequer of public amusement rose to speak. He made a proposal that met with the enthusiastic response of the council. He proposed that the twenty-fifth day of the last month of the year be chosen to publicly honor the grand mayor of Pleasantville. He further suggested that this day be called "Mayor's Day" and that the entire day be spent in honoring His Honor. Only with weak modesty did the mayor protest, so the council voted, and the holiday became official.

170

When the meeting was over, the grand mayor tingled with anticipation: the twenty-fifth day of the last month of the year—*his* day! It seemed to all that he walked a little straighter and carried his chin a little higher. The mayor began to imagine the many congratulations, felicitations, bronzed plaques and plaster awards he would, doubtless, receive. He might even receive some recognition for his past years of selfless service in civic administration. There would also be the joy of watching the town fathers hang up his picture in stores on Main Street. And what exhilaration to hear the community glee club sing "For He's a Jolly Good Mayor" and "He's a Grand Old Mayor."

Soon the excited little town began making ready for Mayor's Day. They hung tinsel and lights between lampposts in the small shopping district. They stretched a giant banner across the street by the town hall which read, "Merry Mayor's Day." Pleasantville Supermarket began to fill its parking lot with fir trees and displayed big signs that said

> Buy Your Mayor's Day Trees from Us!
> 4-foot trees $1.98
> 6-foot trees $2.98
> 8-foot trees $3.98

The mayor failed to see how trees were connected to his day, but he didn't really object, seeing that everyone seemed to be having a great time buying trees and wishing each other a merry Mayor's Day.

Every day the mayor rose early and dressed so the photographers could come and take his picture to be on displays all over town. However, day after day passed, and the photographers did not come. In distress, he called them about his picture. They explained that although they regretted it deeply, they would not be able to come and take his picture. As there were only twenty-one more shopping days left until Mayor's Day, they were pressed for time.

About this time, the mayor began to notice that several other things had gone wrong. For instance, he noticed that one of the civic organizations was having a Mayor's Day *cocktail party.* He had always been against that sort of thing and stood proud of his reputation as a complete teetotaler.

It soon became evident that Mayor's Day celebrations had gone amiss. He had expected people to make speeches in his honor, but nothing of the sort happened. However, someone did write a poem. The poem had nothing to do with the mayor but was instead about a jolly old St. Someone or other. It read:

> 'Twas the night before Mayor's Day
> And all through the house
> Not a creature was stirring,
> Not even a rodent.

They read the poem night and day on Radio Pleasantville.

Nor were any of the songs of the season about the mayor himself. They sang songs like "Sled Ride," "Dingling Bells," "Wonder Winterland," "I'm Dreaming of a White Mayor's Day," and "Rudolph, the Red-Nosed Moose." More of their songs seemed to be in honor of a jolly round saint than in honor of the mayor. In fact, the only thing that seemed to be consistent about everyone's unaccountable behavior was that they all began buying nuts. That, according to the mayor, seemed appropriate.

Finally, Mayor's Day came. The mayor sat alone the whole day, and hardly anyone remembered to call. They

172

were far too busy unwrapping presents to make a visit. They were all gathered in their small separate houses to celebrate their small and separate holidays. And when the plump, steaming Mayor's Day turkey, with cranberries and giblet dumplings, was set on the table, they forced all thoughts of the mayor out of their minds. They knew it would be better not to think about the lonely, forgotten mayor, since they would not really be able to enjoy dinner while entertaining such thoughts.

Most of the citizenry were content to sit under their Mayor's Day trees eating nuts and wishing each other a merry Mayor's Day. And, except for the Mayor, they all gave the impression that they were living happily ever after.

No Shot Was Ever Heard

*This selection, taken from one of my earlier poems,
speaks of my unwillingness to look at Jesus' birth except
through the spectacles of his ultimate victory.*

No shot was ever heard around the world.
In fact, in all of human history
Only two sounds have been heard around the entire
    world.
The first:
A newborn baby's cry, saying, "It is begun."
The second:
A young man's dying cry, saying,
"It is finished."

ANTHEM OF THE STAR

This brief carol is taken from The Legend of the
Brotherstone, *a mythical examination of how God felt
about Christmas.*

Here is the Festival of Stars!
Now reigns our once and glorious King!
Come and behold him
Whose splendor is light—
Whose scepter is joyous day—
Whose coming dispels the gathering night—
Whose chariots fly where the bright planets play!
Come children, come all!
Now gather! Now sing!
For this is the Day of the King!

Once in Every Universe

This small anthem expresses the heartbreak of a God
who was more anxious to communicate his love than his
terror to an already frightened world.

Once in every universe
Some world is worry-torn
And hungry for a global lullaby.
O rest, poor race, and hurtle on through space—
God has umbilicated himself to straw,
Laid by his thunderbolts and learned to cry.